W9-AAV-677

**Contemporary Discourse
in the Field of
PHYSICS** ™

Sound and Electromagnetic Waves

An Anthology of Current Thought

Edited by L. C. Krysac, Ph.D.

The Rosen Publishing Group, Inc., New York

Published in 2006 by The Rosen Publishing Group, Inc.
29 East 21st Street, New York, NY 10010

First Edition

Library of Congress Cataloging-in-Publication Data

Sound and electromagnetic waves: an anthology of current
thought/edited by L. C. Krysac.
     p. cm.—(Contemporary discourse in the field of physics)
Includes bibliographical references and index.
ISBN 1-4042-0407-5 (library binding)
1. Sound-waves. 2. Electromagnetic waves. I. Krysac, L. C. II. Series.
QC243.S68 2005
534—dc22
                                                                    2004026363

Manufactured in the United States of America

On the cover (clockwise from top right): Patterns of light on a
white surface; wave refraction experiment simulating Snell's law,
in which an electromagnetic beam emerges on the same side of a
normal surface as the incident beam; portrait of Sir Issac Newton;
liquid crystal.

CONTENTS

Introduction

A wave is a disturbance that transports energy away from its source. We all have some experience with water waves. Expanding ripples from a dropped pebble serve as an analogy for the reflections, refractions, and diffractions of those waves that affect us but that we cannot see, electromagnetic waves and sound waves. Most waves have some medium through which the wave moves, leaving the medium untouched behind it. An apparent exception to this is the electromagnetic wave, which can travel through the vacuum of space without being supported by any medium. Ordinary light, which we use to image our surroundings, is an electromagnetic wave, a propagating disturbance of the local electric and magnetic fields. Sound waves always have a medium, the most familiar being air, which carries sounds that we hear with our ears. Sound waves can be carried in any substance, like water (not to be confused with water waves), in bone or metal, and in the rocks beneath Earth's surface.

Both electromagnetic and sound waves can propagate with wavelengths or frequencies too large or too small for humans to detect directly. The electromagnetic spectrum extends far beyond the visible wavelengths into the ultraviolet, where wavelengths of first X-rays and then gamma rays become smaller and smaller (high frequencies), and deep into the infrared, where one finds the long wavelengths of microwaves, television broadcasting, and radio waves (low frequencies). Similarly, sounds with frequencies below about 20 hertz (Hz), called infrasound, and sounds with frequencies above 20,000 Hz, called ultrasound, are inaudible to human ears. Scientists and engineers have explored and exploited in various technologies the full range of both spectrums, electromagnetic and acoustic.

The study of sound waves has a long history. Aristotle (384–322 BC) noted that sound was generated by air motion, as did Pythagoras (c. 550 BC). Other early philosophers likewise suggested that sound had properties similar to those of waves. The laws for the natural frequencies of vibrating strings were deduced by Marin Mersenne (1588–1648), a French natural philosopher, and by Galileo Galilei (1564–1642). Isaac Newton (1642–1727) presented a mechanical interpretation of sound as a "pressure" pulse transmitted from one particle to the next in a fluid. Since then, the study of sound, or acoustics, has been pursued by many great scientists, and the wave theory of sound has been developed to a highly advanced level.

Today, acoustics is studied and applied by scientists and engineers in a far-ranging selection of fields—physics, geophysics, measurement technologies, noise control, structural vibrations, aeronautics, oceanography, biology, animal acoustics, physiology, psychology, architectural acoustics, speech, hearing, and musical acoustics, for example. The selection of articles presented in this anthology gives a small sampling of the exciting advances taking place in some of these fields.

The secrets of the hidden Earth and the structure of boundaries between Earth's molten core and the surrounding rock are being uncovered by geophysicists studying the reflection and diffraction of seismic waves produced by earthquakes. The exciting possibilities suggested by the recently discovered phenomenon of sonoluminescence, where sound excites the collapse of tiny bubbles to produce flashes of light, are being explored. The effects of infrasound and ultrasound on humans, the acoustics of concert halls and underwater creatures, and new heat engine technologies made possible by the exploitation of sound waves are all subjects of current research in the science of sound waves.

Electromagnetic waves have a shorter but equally rich history. The nature of light as an electromagnetic wave was only understood at the end of the 1800s, after several hundred years of scientific exploration. Hans Oersted (1777–1851) carried out experiments in the 1820s that related electric current with magnetic fields, an idea that was reinforced by the experiments of André Marie Ampère (1775–1836). In the 1830s, Michael Faraday (1791–1867) and Joseph Henry (1797–1878) discovered the basis of the electrical generator—electrical induction, in which a changing magnetic field creates an electric field inside a conductor. These experiments were the basis for the theories, written in 1864, of James Clerk Maxwell (1831–1879), which stated that light was a wave where electric and magnetic fields oscillated together. Twenty years later, his theories were proven correct by experiments performed by Heinrich Hertz (1857–1894).

These pioneering works established that electromagnetic radiation is a wave that travels through space at the speed of light, with an electric field component that oscillates in strength while always pointing perpendicular to the direction of travel. The magnetic field does likewise, while also remaining perpendicular to the electric field. Electromagnetic waves are generated by any oscillation of electric charge, and as waves, they can be reflected, diffracted, and refracted. Also as waves, they carry energy, a fact that has been exploited by humans to create the global communications network of radio and television, for example.

To create radio waves, such as those emitted by a cellular phone, electric charges are accelerated up and down a conductor, called an antenna. Similarly, to detect radio waves, the energy in the electromagnetic wave accelerates charges in an antenna, creating an electrical signal that can be transformed into sound. Modern antennas are, therefore, key elements for communication and are a highly evolved technology, as described in one of the selections in this anthology.

In addition, other selections describe applications of electromagnetic radiation for digital data storage, optical electronics and communications, testing and measurement in the semiconductor industry, materials characterization, and biological analysis. These articles, most of which are written by scientists and engineers who have firsthand experience with the subjects, show that the discovery of electromagnetic waves has been one of the most important for human technological progress. They also show that the potential for new technology based on electromagnetic waves is practically infinite and is perpetually being explored. *—LCK*

1

Waves in the Natural World

Earth has an interior structure. The uppermost layer is a thin, hard crust that floats on a convective layer of hot rock called the mantle. Beneath the mantle is the molten core, which surrounds a solid inner core. How can scientists know this about Earth, when it's impossible to drill through the 19-mile-thick (31-kilometer-thick) crust alone? The answer is that by observing the sound waves produced by earthquakes and using the knowledge of how waves reflect, refract, and diffract, the structure deep below Earth's surface can be deduced. The study of these seismic waves is called "seismology," and "seismic tomography" produces images of slices of Earth's interior.

Different properties of waves are used in the interpretation of data recorded at seismic stations around the world. For example, seismic waves can be P waves, which are compressional waves, or S waves, which are shear waves. The P waves can travel through solids and fluids, but S waves can travel only through solids. S waves, *for instance, cannot travel through Earth's fluid core. Seismologists also use the fact that the speed and attenuation of sound waves in any material depends on the material's elastic properties, the ease with which it stretches and compresses. When a seismic wave, or any sound wave, passes through a place where those properties vary, that place is the location of an elastic heterogeneity.*

In this article, professors Thorne Lay and Quentin Williams (Earth Sciences Department, University of California, Santa Cruz) and Professor Edward J. Garnero (Seismological Laboratory, University of California, Berkeley) review the observations and interpretations of seismic waves reflecting from the boundary between the hard mantle and the soft core, the core-mantle boundary (CMB). Through decades of study, seismologists have discovered that this region of Earth's interior is rich with interesting features. —LCK

From "The Core-Mantle Boundary Layer and Deep Earth Dynamics"
by Thorne Lay, Quentin Williams, and Edward J. Garnero
Nature, April 2, 1998

Recent seismological work has revealed new structures in the boundary layer between the Earth's core and mantle that are altering and expanding perspectives of the role this region plays in both core and mantle dynamics. Clear challenges for future research in seismological, experimental, theoretical and computational geophysics have emerged, holding the key to understanding both this dynamic system and geological phenomena observed at the Earth's surface.

The Earth acquired its primary layered structure—consisting of a molten metallic alloy core overlaid by a thick shell of silicates and oxides—very early in its history, and the region near the core-mantle boundary (CMB) surface has undoubtedly played a significant role in both the core and mantle dynamic systems throughout their subsequent 4.5-Gyr evolution. The CMB has a density contrast exceeding that found at the surface of the Earth, has contrasts in viscosity and physical state comparable to those at the ocean floor, and has much hotter ambient temperatures than found near the surface.[1, 2] These factors, together with the requirement that significant heat be flowing from the core into the mantle in order to sustain the geodynamo (the core magnetohydrodynamic flow regime that produces the Earth's magnetic field), provide the basis for the conventional view that a significant thermal boundary layer exists at the base of the mantle, with a temperature contrast of $1,000 \pm 500$ K (refs 2–4). With ambient temperatures averaging around 3,000 K, this hot thermal boundary layer is a likely source of boundary-layer instabilities, and it has been speculated that upwelling thermal plumes ascend from the CMB to produce surface hotspot volcanism such as at Hawaii and Iceland, transporting about 10–15 % of the surface heat flux.[5-7] The large CMB density contrast favours a mantle-side accumulation of chemical heterogeneities derived from initial and continuing chemical differentiation of the mantle, possibly including downwelling subducted slabs of former oceanic lithosphere; distinctive chemical signatures of these heterogeneities may eventually be entrained into thermal plumes, resulting in unique hotspot chemistry.[8, 9] There may also be a core-side chemical and thermal boundary layer, but the low seismic velocities and molten state of the core make it much harder to analyse any structure in the outermost core.[2]

In the past decade, seismic tomography has provided steadily improving images of deep mantle elastic velocity heterogeneity, revealing the presence of significant large-scale (> 2,000 km) patterns of coherent high- and low-velocity regions at all depths,[10-12] with enhanced lateral variations in the lowermost 300 km. Attributing the seismological variations to lateral thermal and chemical heterogeneity in the boundary layer suggests several mechanisms of coupling between the core and mantle, influencing the core flow regime as well as irregularities in rotation of the planet.[2, 13-15] An experimental demonstration that chemical reactions may be continuing between the core and mantle has raised the possibility of electromagnetic coupling across the boundary.[16, 17] These considerations assign possible importance to the CMB layer for dynamic processes throughout the planet (including an intimate relationship to surface structures), yet the precise role of the CMB region remains a topic of vigorous research and debate requiring improved resolution of the structure and processes operating there.

Several recent seismological discoveries have revealed new attributes of the mantle-side boundary layer overlying the CMB. The lowermost 200 km of the mantle (known as the D″ region) has long been characterized by seismologists as distinctive in its properties from the overlying deep mantle. Numerous studies have revealed the presence of intermittent stratification of the D″ region in many areas, with 1.5–3 % velocity discontinuities for both compressional (P) and shear (S) waves at depths of 150–300 km above the CMB;[18–21] studies have also shown the presence of laterally varying shear-wave anisotropy (birefringence that splits the S waves into orthogonal polarizations that travel with different velocities owing to organized mineralogical or petrographical fabrics) in the D″ region that is, at least sometimes, related to the discontinuity structure.[22–26] Both observations lack satisfactory explanations in terms of current understanding of thermal and mineralogical structure of the deep mantle. A newly discovered laterally varying ultra-low-velocity layer in the lowermost few tens of kilometres of the mantle[27–29] is also challenging the conventional view, as the magnitude of the velocity drop (10 % or more reductions in both P and S velocities) is so large that it probably involves partial melting of the mantle, with attendant broad implications for chemical reactions, heat transport, and boundary-layer dynamics.[29] Together with the latest generation of high-spatial-resolution seismic tomography images,[30, 31] these seismic observations and their spatial systematics raise many questions about primary processes in the CMB boundary layer that define challenging research frontiers for experimental and computational geophysics. The present state of knowledge about the CMB region parallels that of the lithospheric boundary layer in the early 1960s, at the dawn of the plate-tectonics revolution. It is reasonable to expect that a concerted effort to quantify the deep boundary layer processes will achieve large advances in our understanding of the dynamic Earth system.

Seismological Discoveries

The elastic velocity structure of the lowermost mantle has been studied by seismologists for decades,[32] yet an important new discovery of some fundamental aspect of the structure in the D″ region has occurred every few years. Although traditional arrival-time analysis procedures for seismic P and S waves continue to lie at the heart of the increasing resolution of seismic tomography models, detailed analysis of waveforms for a variety of secondary phases has played a larger role in revealing high-resolution details of the boundary-layer structure.

Figure 1 illustrates some of the ray paths associated with seismic phases that provide information about the deep mantle structure. P and S waves that graze the D″ region (Fig. 1a), either reflecting off of the core (PcP, ScS) or diffracting along it (P_{diff}, S_{diff}) have been studied for decades, but recent analysis procedures which account for shallow mantle effects are revealing coherent large-scale patterns that augment those detected by travel-time tomography.[33] Commonly, differential anomalies such as ScS–S arrival times are used to help isolate lower-mantle contributions. The discovery in the early 1980s of a deep-mantle shear-wave reflector several hundred kilometres above the CMB[34] introduced the analysis of reflections and refractions (S_{bc} and S_{cd} in Fig. 1b, and their P-wave counterparts), which are used to map the lateral extent of localized stratification and its depth and material property contrasts. Core-grazing and core-reflected S waves can also be analysed for any shear-wave splitting associated with anisotropic structure near the base of the mantle, although shallow mantle effects need to be accounted for carefully. For examining the seismic properties within tens of kilometres of the CMB, the optimal seismic waves are short-period P reflections (PcP) and S to P conversions (ScP), as well as longer-period S waves that convert at the CMB, transmitting through or diffracting along the CMB as P waves, before they travel back to the surface as S waves (SKS and SPdKS phases in Fig. 1c). PKP phases and their scattered precursors also provide critical information about small-scale structures in D″. . . .

Figure 1 Seismic-wave ray-paths from a deep focus source (circle) to a receiver (triangle) for phases that have been extensively used to image the velocity structure of the deep mantle. **a,** Core-grazing phases such as the reflection ScS, direct S near 90°, and diffracted S (S_{diff}) in the shadow zone. These have P-wave counterparts. Grazing waves provide sensitivity to lateral heterogeneity and anisotropy in the D″ region. **b,** D″ triplication phases, including reflections (S_{bc}) and refractions (S_{cd}) from a velocity discontinuity. These have P-wave counterparts. Triplications constrain the depth and strength of any discontinuities. **c,** Phases used to study the ULVZ include short-period reflections (PcP) and conversions (ScP), as well as the long-period SKS phase and its associated SPdKS phase (involving P energy diffracted along the core).

Figure 1

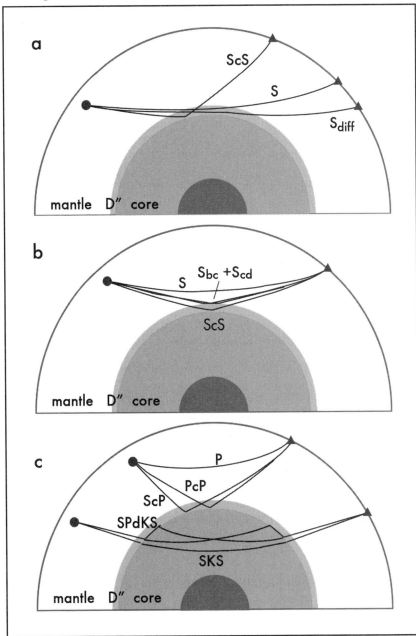

The rapidity with which new structures within D″ have been seismically characterized has (for the moment) outpaced the corresponding interpretive geodynamic and experimental work. Indeed, few studies have been conducted to date which were designed to constrain the nature of the newly discovered seismic structures of this region. Because of the importance of this region, and because of the temporary offset between the observations and interpretive studies—coupled with the accelerating number and enhanced quality of seismic observations—it seems likely that the CMB is about to replace the transition zone between Earth's upper and lower mantle as the region most likely to hold the key to a large number of geophysical problems.[93]

References

1. Lay, T. Structure of the core-mantle transition zone: A chemical and thermal boundary layer. *Eos* **70**, 54–55, 58–59 (1989).

2. Loper, D. E. & Lay, T. The core-mantle boundary region. *J. Geophys. Res.* **100**, 6397–6420 (1995).

3. Williams, Q. & Jeanloz, R. Melting relations in the iron-sulfur system at high pressures: Implications for the thermal state of the Earth. *J. Geophys. Res.* **95**, 19299–19310 (1990).

4. Boehler, R. Temperatures in the Earth's core from melting-point measurements of iron at high static pressures. *Nature* **363**, 534-536 (1993).

5. Davies, G. F. Ocean bathymetry and mantle convection, 1, Large-scale flow and hotspots. *J. Geophys. Res.* **93**, 10447–10480 (1988).

6. Sleep, N. H. Hotspots and mantle plumes: Some phenomenology. *J. Geophys. Res.* **95**, 6715–6736 (1990).

7. Loper, D. E. Mantle plumes. *Tectonophysics* **187**, 373-384 (1991).

8. Hoffman, A. W. & White, W. M. Mantle plumes from ancient oceanic crust. *Earth Planet. Sci. Lett.* **57**, 421–436 (1982).

9. Woodhead, J. D., Greenwood, P., Harmon, R. S. & Stoffers, P. Oxygen isotope evidence for recycled crust in the source of EM-type ocean island basalts. *Nature* **362**, 809–813 (1993).

10. Su, W-J., Woodward, R. & Dziewonski, A. M. Degree 12 model of shear velocity heterogeneity in the mantle. *J. Geophys. Res.* **99**, 6945–6980 (1994).

11. Li, X. D. & Romanowicz, B. Global mantle shear velocity model developed using nonlinear asymptotic coupling theory. *J. Geophys. Res.* **101**, 22245–22272 (1996).

12. Masters, T. G., Johnson, S., Laske, G. & Bolton, H. A shear-velocity model of the mantle. *Phil. Trans. R. Soc. Lond.* A **354**, 1385–1411 (1996).

13. Gubbins, D. Core-mantle interactions. *Tectonophysics* **187**, 385–391 (1991).

14. Bloxham, J. & Jackson, A. Fluid flow near the surface of Earth's outer core. *Rev. Geophys.* **29**, 97–120 (1991).

15. Hide, R., Speith, M. A., Clayton, R. W., Hager, B. H. & Voorhies, C. V. in *Relating Geophysical Structures and Processes: The Jeffreys Volume* (eds Aki, K. & Dmowska, R.) 107–120 (Geophys. Monogr. Ser. 76, Am. Geophys Union, Washington DC, 1993).

16. Knittle, E. & Jeanloz, R. Earth's core-mantle boundary: Results of experiments at high pressures and temperatures. *Science* **251**, 1438–1443 (1991).

17. Poirier, J.-P. Core-infiltrated mantle and the nature of the D″ layer. *J. Geomagn. Geoelectr.* **45**, 1221–1227 (1993).

18. Lay, T. Seismology of the lower mantle and core-mantle boundary. *Rev. Geophys. Suppl.* 325–328 (1995).

19. Weber, M. *et al.* in *Seismic Modeling of the Earth's Structure* (eds Boschi, E., Ekström, G. & Morelli, A.) 399–442 (Istit. Naz. di Geophys., Rome, 1996).

20. Ding, X. & Helmberger, D. V. Modeling D″ structure beneath Central America with broadband seismic data. *Phys. Earth Planet Inter.* **101**, 245–270 (1997).

21. Wysession, M. E. *et al.* The D″ discontinuity and its implications. in *The Core-Mantle Boundary* (eds Gurnis, M., Buffett, B. A., Knittle, E. & Wysession, M.) (Am. Geophys. Union, in the press).

22. Vinnik, L., Romanowicz, B., Le Stunff, Y. & Makeyeva, L. Seismic anisotropy in the D″ layer. *Geophys. Res. Lett.* **22**, 1657–1660 (1995).

23. Kendall, J.-M. & Silver, P. G. Constraints from seismic anisotropy on the nature of the lowermost mantle. *Nature* **381**, 409-412 (1996).

24. Matzel, E., Sen, M. K. & Grand, S. P. Evidence for anisotropy in the deep mantle beneath Alaska. *Geophys. Res. Lett.* **23**, 2417–2420 (1996).

25. Garnero, E. J. & Lay, T. Lateral variations in lowermost mantle shear wave anisotropy beneath the north Pacific and Alaska. *J. Geophys. Res.* **102**, 8121–8135 (1997).

26. Lay, T., Garnero, E. J., Williams, Q., Kellogg, L. & Wysession, M. E. Seismic wave anisotropy in the D″ region and its implications. in *The Core-Mantle Boundary* (eds Gurnis, M., Buffett, B. A., Knittle, E. & Wysession, M.) (Am. Geophys. Union, in the press).

27. Garnero, E. J. & Helmberger, D. V. A very slow basal layer underlying large-scale low-velocity anomalies in the lower mantle beneath the Pacific: evidence from core phases. *Phys. Earth Planet. Inter.* **91**, 161–176 (1995).

28. Mori, J. & Helmberger, D. V. Localized boundary layer below the mid-Pacific velocity anomaly identified from a PcP precursor. *J. Geophys. Res.* **100**, 20359–20365 (1995).

29. Garnero, E. J., Revenaugh, J., Williams, Q., Lay, T. & Kellogg, L. Ultra-low velocity zone at the core-mantle boundary. in *The Core-Mantle Boundary* (eds Gurnis, M., Buffett, B. A., Knittle, E. & Wysession, M.) (Am Geophys. Union, in the press).

30. Grand, S. P., van der Hilst, R. D. & Widiyantoro, S. Global seismic tomography: A snapshot of convection in the Earth. *GSA Today* **7**, 1–7 (1997).

31. van der Hilst, R. D., Widiyantoro, S. & Engdahl, E. R. Evidence for deep mantle circulation from global tomography. *Nature* **386**, 578–584 (1997).

32. Young, C. J. & Lay, T. The core mantle boundary. *Annu. Rev. Earth Planet. Sci.* **15**, 25–46 (1987).

33. Wysession, M. E. Large scale structure at the core-mantle boundary from core-diffracted waves. *Nature* **382**, 244–248 (1996).

34. Lay, T. & Helmberger, D. V. A lower mantle S-wave triplication and the shear velocity structure of D". *Geophys. J. R. Astron. Soc.* **75**, 799–838 (1983).

93. Birch, F. Elasticity and constitution of the Earth's interior. *J. Geophys. Res.* **57**, 227–286 (1952).

The rainbow is a beautiful example of light interacting with matter, reflecting and refracting as it passes through raindrops. John Hardwick, manager of the lightning division of Culham Electromagnetics and Lightning, Ltd., in Abingdon, England, uses simple geometry to explain why a rainbow always appears the way it does, in the same way to each of us no matter where we are standing when we see one. It's not obvious why it should be this way,

when the air can be full of many different raindrops and there can be many possibilities for reflection and refraction of the sunlight. Why does only a particular set of reflections at a particular angle reach our eyes?

In addition to the commonly seen primary rainbow, many people have seen the secondary rainbow, and a few privileged people (myself included) have seen the much rarer tertiary rainbow. This article explains where to look to see all these bows when the air is damp with rain. —LCK

From "The Subtlety of Rainbows"
by John Hardwick
Physics World, February 2004

In his poem of 1820 entitled *Lamia*, John Keats complained that cold philosophy had destroyed the mystery of nature, and that Newton, through his work on optics, had "unweave[d the] rainbow." Such a sentiment would find little sympathy with most scientists—or with most artists today for that matter. Indeed, an understanding of natural phenomena can only enhance our appreciation of nature and art.

Although it has long been known that a rainbow is produced by the dispersion of white light through rain droplets via refraction, there is far more to this optical phenomenon than first meets the eye. More complex and subtle interactions between light and water droplets can also create the "fog-bow," the "dew-bow" and the "glory."

Rainbows Explained

Despite being a familiar sight, rainbows are much harder to understand than one might think. The ingredients are, of course, sunlight and rain droplets. Although the Sun's rays that reach the Earth are essentially parallel, the light impinges on a spherical droplet at a wide range of angles to the surface, where it undergoes refraction. When the light reaches the back of the droplet, two things can happen (figure 2*a* [in original article]). The light can either refract and continue in a forward direction out of the drop, or it can be reflected internally, before passing back out through the front surface of the droplet via another refraction. It is this second process—in which light is refracted, reflected and refracted again—that creates the rainbow, which explains why rainbows only appear when one looks away from the Sun into a rain shower.

There are, however, innumerable raindrops at many different heights and positions above the horizon. As a result—and because of the many different angles at which the sunlight strikes the droplets' surfaces—we receive light rays at many different angles to the "antisolar direction," which is the direction looking away from the Sun towards the shadow of our head. So why does the bright, coloured arc of the rainbow only appear centred on this direction and at a specific and narrow range of angles to it?

Consider first what happens when the incident light strikes the surface of a droplet head on. Some of the light continues straight through the drop, while the rest reflects directly back. For the latter, the "angle of deviation" between the incident and reflected beams is 180°. But as the incident light strikes the droplet at a larger angle, the angle of deviation falls below 180°. When the incident light strikes at even larger angles, the deviation eventually reaches a minimum value, before rising again [see page 25].

At the minimum-deviation angle the rate of change of deviation angle with incident angle is zero. What this means is that light striking a droplet over a relatively wide range of incident angles emerges concentrated in a narrow—and almost parallel—direction. For example, light rays spanning a 13° interval around the incident angle for minimum deviation are focused down to an emerging beam with an angular width of just 1°. Light travelling in this direction has a relatively high intensity and forms part of the standard—or "primary"—rainbow with which we are all familiar.

Different colours have slightly different minimum deviation angles; it is about 140° for short-wavelength violet light and falls to 138° for red light. The violet component of a primary rainbow is therefore on the bow's inner side—about 40° to the antisolar direction—while the red component is on the outside at about 42° (figure 2c). Other colours fall in between. As the Sun rises, all that changes is that we see less and less of the rainbow's arc as the "antisolar point"—the centre of the circle of which the rainbow is a part—and the outer limbs of the bow gradually sink below the horizon. Interestingly, if the Sun is higher than 42° above the horizon, minimum-deviation rays can only be received from drops located at angles below it, which is why rainbows are generally not visible when the Sun is high in the sky at the middle of the day.

Another interesting property of a primary rainbow is that the intensity of light coming from below it is higher than the background intensity from above it . . . The reason for this is that rain droplets cannot contribute to any light coming from angles above the rainbow because light cannot be bent round a droplet by less than the minimum angle of deviation. Some of the light scattered by the raindrop can, however, reach the observer from below the rainbow, which is therefore brighter than the area above it—but of course, not nearly as bright as the rainbow itself.

Although a large proportion of light exits the drops after a single internal reflection to form the primary rainbow, some light can undergo two internal reflections.

Figure 2 Rainbow optics. (a) A parallel beam of sunlight striking a spherical rain droplet. Despite being parallel, the light strikes the droplet at a wide range of different angles. The light undergoes refraction as it enters the droplet before undergoing reflection and further refraction. (b) The "angle of deviation" (top line) between the incoming and outgoing rays passes through a minimum value for each wavelength, which is 138° for red light. The intensity of the deviated light (bottom line) reaches a maximum at this angle and is responsible for the creation of a "primary" rainbow. (c) Different colours have different minimum-deviation angles because the refractive index of water depends on wavelength. The angle between light from the primary rainbow and the "antisolar direction" is 42° for the red bow and 40° for the violet bow. A separate, less intense "secondary" bow can also be created from light that undergoes not one but two reflections from inside the droplet. The colours of this bow appear in reverse order to the primary bow.

Figure 2

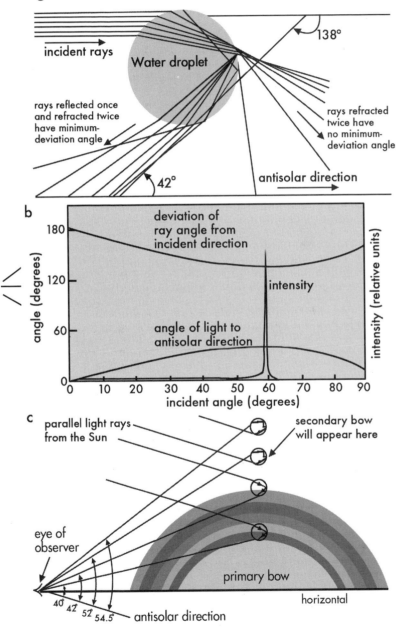

Such twice-reflected rays, which also have minimum-deviation angles and associated intensity maxima, form a "secondary" bow. This appears above the primary bow at an angle of about 52° to the antisolar direction. The secondary bow is fainter than the primary bow and the colours appear in the reverse order . . .

What about those light rays that pass out through the droplets in the forward direction after two refractions and no reflection? These have no minimum deviation, which means that this light does not reach a maximum intensity at any particular angle. In other words, if we look towards the Sun through rain, we will see no bright rainbow but just an overall forward glare.

However, in principle, a "tertiary" bow can also be formed after the light has undergone three internal reflections in a droplet. This would occur when looking towards the Sun at an angle of about 40°, but it would be fainter than the secondary bow and obscured by forward glare. There have been some reported sightings of a tertiary bow . . . but no photographs exist, so far at least! . . .

Keats' Unweaved Rainbow

So has cold philosophy unweaved the rainbow? It seems to me that a fuller understanding of the physical basis of this intricate phenomenon can lead to a proper appreciation of it and also shed light on other, yet more subtle effects that lie outside what Keats called the "dull catalogue of common things." Each rainbow, halo and glory is unique in that each results from a never-to-be-repeated ensemble of raindrops or ice crystals of particular shapes and sizes. Some forms, like the Whymper apparition, are so rare that you will be lucky to ever see one in your lifetime.

The physics of the rainbow is perhaps like particle physics, in that each deeper explanation reveals yet another mystery. However, unlike particle physics, we have the final word with Mie scattering theory, which as well as explaining the glory gives a complete theory of the rainbow. But questions still persist. Why, for example, are dew-bows so rare? And why does lightning destroy a rainbow? It appears that some subtleties surrounding the rainbow continue to remain a mystery.

Reprinted with permission from *Physics World*.

2 Waves in Human Constructions

The collapse of the Tacoma Narrows Bridge in Puget Sound near Tacoma, Washington, on November 7, 1940, has been used in classrooms as a classic example of "resonance," when waves in a solid object group together to make large-amplitude oscillations. A more familiar example of resonance due to forced oscillations might be pushing a child on a swing, where pushing at just the right time intervals, at just the right frequency, results in the child and swing reaching greater and greater swinging heights. In the case of the Tacoma Narrows Bridge, the external forcing agent was the wind rushing down the narrows, creating vortices of air peeling from the bridge as it rushed past. The resulting wild oscillations eventually destroyed the bridge.

In this article, Professor Bernard J. Feldman of the University of Missouri–St. Louis decries the misleading explanations put forth by educators and in textbooks, and then gives a more detailed and more correct *explanation. The details he examines include the forced oscillations due to the wind shedding vortices from the bridge, as well as more compli-cated and fascinating torsional oscillations, the source and amplification of which are still being debated among engineers. —LCK*

From "What to Say About the Tacoma Narrows Bridge to Your Introductory Physics Class"
by Bernard J. Feldman
The Physics Teacher, February 2003

Having just taught my introductory physics class about the collapse of the Tacoma Narrows Bridge, I realized that this topic is fascinating both to the students and to me. I always show the video and it never fails to elicit numerous questions from the class. However, its treatment in most introductory physics textbooks is either at best inadequate or at worst mis-leading. By chance, I also recently heard a talk from the project manager of a proposed new bridge across the Mississippi River at St. Louis. The issues that led to the failure of the Tacoma Narrows Bridge played a major role in the design of this new bridge. These two events have led me to think about the physics of bridge oscillations and to write this paper, which is in large part an abridged version of the 1991 *American Journal of Physics* article by Billah and Scanlan,[1] but it is clear to me that the content of that article has not permeated the physics community.

Tacoma Narrows Bridge
Vertical Oscillations

If you watch the video of the collapse of the Tacoma Narrows Bridge,[2] you will observe two very different types of bridge oscillation. Up until an hour before the collapse of the bridge, the only observed oscillation was a vertical motion of the bridge deck. This vertical oscillation is an example of simple forced harmonic oscillation—the sinusoidal motion of the deck due to an external sinusoidal force . . .

This steady-state solution displays two defining characteristics of forced harmonic motion. One is that the bridge deck oscillates at ω_{ex}, the angular frequency of the external sinusoidal force, not at ω_0, the natural angular frequency of the bridge bed. Second, the amplitude of the oscillation has a maximum when $\omega_{ex} = \omega_0$ (in other words, a resonance behavior as a function of wind velocity since ω_{ex} is proportional to the wind velocity).

The vertical oscillations of a model Tacoma Narrows Bridge in a wind tunnel display both characteristics of forced harmonic motion. First, the frequency of the vertical oscillations varies linearly with the wind velocity. Second, Fig. 1 shows the amplitude of various oscillations as a function of wind velocity; notice that curves 1-NV and 2-NV show the expected resonance behavior.[3]

The oscillating external force involved in these vertical oscillations is due to vortex shedding by the constant velocity wind separated by the deck of the bridge. These vortex arrays, commonly called a Karman

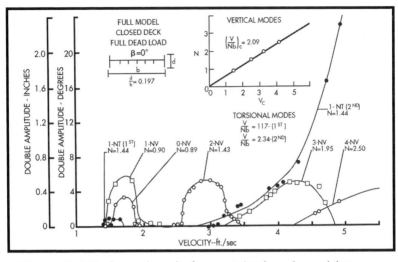

Figure 1. Wind-tunnel results from a 1/50th-scale model Tacoma Narrows Bridge.[3] The wind velocity in the wind tunnel of 5 ft/s (1.5 m/s) is equivalent to a wind velocity of 35 mph (16 m/s) for a full-size bridge.

vortex street and sketched in Fig. 2, are two rows of vortices with opposite directions of circulation and with a frequency that is approximately proportional to the wind velocity. At the time a vortex breaks loose from the top (bottom) of the bridge deck, a downward (upward) force is exerted on the bridge deck, as sketched in Fig. 2.

A number of everyday occurrences are explained by this phenomenon of vortex shedding. For example, automobile radio antennae will oscillate perpendicular to the motion of a car at certain resonant velocities. In heavy winds, stoplights strung across streets will oscillate perpendicular to the direction of the wind. A simple classroom demonstration of vortex shedding is

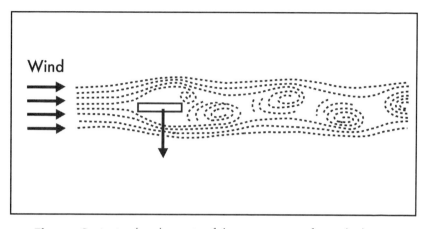

Figure 2. A simple schematic of the vortex array formed when a constant wind blows around a bridge deck.[2] The downward arrow is the direction of the force exerted on the deck by the creation of the vortex above the bridge deck.

the motion of a sheet of paper that is dropped to the floor; each flutter of the paper is one vortex being shed.

Tacoma Narrow Bridge Torsional Oscillations

In the last 45 minutes of the life of the Tacoma Narrows Bridge, a new twisting, torsional motion is observed, which has a very large amplitude and is the cause of the bridge's collapse. This oscillation is an aerodynamically induced self-excitation (or aerodynamic flutter). The solution to Newton's second law for a self-excited system also gives a steady-state sinusoidal solution. The two characteristics of this steady-state solution are motion at the natural frequency ω_0 (not at ω_{ex}, since there is no external sinusoidal torque), and no resonance behavior in the amplitude as a function of the wind velocity. The torsional motion of the model Tacoma Narrows Bridge in a wind tunnel has both these characteristics. First, the frequency of the torsional motion does not change with wind velocity. Second, returning to Fig. 1, the curve 1-NT is due to the torsional motion and shows no resonance behavior.

A further insight into the self-excited motion comes from the transient solution to Newton's second law. . . . The amplitude of the transient solution is exponential in time, where the exponent is a function of the aerodynamic flutter coefficient, A_2, and the torsional damping coefficient, b. This exponent can be either positive or negative, depending on the magnitude and sign of A_2 and b.

Scanlon and Tomko fitted A_2 to the transient motion of a model Tacoma Narrows Bridge in a wind tunnel.[4] . . . At wind velocities less than 10 mph (4.5 m/s), A_2 is negative, the exponential coefficient is negative, and the torsional motion decays in time. However, above 27 mph (12 m/s), A_2 is positive and greater than b, the exponent becomes positive, and the torsional motion grows exponentially in time. From the video, the Tacoma Narrows Bridge was in a steady-state mode most of the 45 minutes of torsional motion. My guess is that as the wind increased in speed, the amplitude initially grew exponentially, but as the amplitude increased, so did b until a new steady-state amplitude was reached.

The really difficult question is the physical mechanism behind the behavior of A_2. . . . Billah and Scanlon suggest that the torsional motion of the bridge generated a vortex wake that amplified the torsional motion.[1] They call this an "aeronautically induced condition of self-excitation."

However, there are other proposed explanations.[2] Lazer and McKenna proposed a nonlinear model where first the wind drove the bridge cables into a high-frequency oscillation; then a nonlinear mechanism channeled that energy into the low-frequency torsional mode.[5]

The New Mississippi River Bridge

By coincidence, as I was lecturing my class about the Tacoma Narrows Bridge, I heard a talk by Keith Hinkebein from HNTB Corp. about the design of the proposed new Mississippi River Bridge in St. Louis. Hinkebein is the project manager for this endeavor, which is sponsored by the Illinois Department of Transportation and the Missouri Department of Transportation . . . Naturally, I asked him how this bridge had been designed to withstand high winds and tornadoes.

One can first ask what does the simple analysis in this paper suggest about how to improve bridge stability. In the case of forced harmonic oscillations, if the bridge is made much more rigid, the natural frequencies of the bridge can be increased so that they are greater than the Karman wave frequency of very high winds. Consequently, most modern bridges are much more rigid than the Tacoma Narrows Bridge.

In the case of self-excited amplification, the goal is to increase b, so it is greater than any possible A_2. In the case of the new Tacoma Narrows Bridge, hydraulic dampers were installed at the towers and piers to increase b.[6] High torsional stiffness is also essential for bridge stability, since it shifts the self-excited oscillations to much higher wind velocities.[4]

In the case of the new Mississippi River Bridge, the engineers relied on both theory and wind-tunnel measurements to ensure the stability of this bridge. The most serious wind-induced oscillation of this new bridge was an aerodynamic self-excitation mode, just as in the case of the Tacoma Narrows Bridge. The major new design feature used to suppress this self-excitation mode is a wide (12-m) slot between the two decks of the bridge, which tends to equalize the pressure above and below the bridge deck.

What an Instructor Should Say

For all high school and many college physics courses, the treatment in the appendices using differential equations is far too advanced. However, the instructor can give a qualitative explanation as follows: There were two types of oscillation of the Tacoma Narrows Bridge. The vertical oscillation is an example of forced harmonic oscillations, where the vortex train created by the wind separated by the bridge deck is the sinusoidal external force. The major characteristics of forced harmonic oscillation are that the frequency of the vertical oscillation of the bridge deck is at the vortex shedding frequency, and the amplitude of the oscillation has a maximum when the vortex shedding frequency equals the natural vertical frequency of the bridge deck. In contrast, the torsional oscillation is an aerodynamically induced self-excitation phenomenon, where the amplification mechanism is still being debated by engineers. The major characteristics of self-excitation oscillations are that the oscillation frequency is the natural torsional frequency of the bridge deck, and there is no resonance phenomenon in the amplitude as a function of wind velocity.

Conclusions

Billah and Scanlon[1] made a very astute observation in 1991 that is still valid today. They point out that the mystery of the collapse of the Tacoma Narrows Bridge is not a mystery; Farquharson in 1950 gave the correct explanation from wind tunnel studies.[3] The real mystery is why the physics community has not taught the correct explanation for all the years since 1950, and may I add, since the publication of the *AJP* article by Billah and Scanlan in 1991. My hope is that this paper will help end this mystery. My other hope is that the real mystery, the lack of understanding of the physical mechanism for self-excited oscillations, may in a small way inspire future physicists and engineers. My experience is that excitement and interest in physics and engineering is generated not only by what is understood but also by what is not.

References

1. K. Y. Billah and R. H. Scanlon, "Resonance, Tacoma Narrows bridge failure, and undergraduate physics textbooks," *Am. J. Phys.* **59**, 118–124 (Feb. 1991).
2. "Twin Views of the Tacoma Narrows Bridge Collapse," video and user's guide produced by R. G. Fuller, C. R. Lang, and R. H. Lang (AAPT, College Park, MD, 20740).

3. *Aerodynamic Stability of Suspension Bridges*, edited by F. B. Farquharson, University of Washington Engineering Experimental Stations Bulletin, No. 116 (June 1949–June 1954), Parts 1–5.

4. A more detailed mathematical model of a coupled vertical and torsional motion is found in R. H. Scanlon and J. J. Tomko, "Airfoil and bridge deck flutter derivatives," *J. Eng. Mech.* **97**, 1717 (Dec. 1971).

5. I. Peterson, "Rock and roll bridge," *Sci. News* **137**, 344 (June 1990).

6. J. Koughan at http://www.me.utexas.edu/~uer/paper_jk.html.

Why does one concert hall make an orchestra sound wonderful, while the same orchestra in another hall might sound dry and pale? Acoustical scientists and engineers have tried to answer that question and then design concert halls in accordance with the laws of acoustics. Modern concert hall designers attempt to control the sound with adjustable panels and resonant spaces, yet the results are not always as success-ful as we might hope.

Music is a complicated cultural expression, and the place where music is played greatly affects the listeners' experience. In this article, written by New York Times critic Edward Rothstein, the effects of attempting to control the technical quality of the sound of a concert hall through acoustical engineering is discussed and criticized. Although science helps us understand so much about our world, it appears that our experience of music remains something more

Sound and Electromagnetic Waves

personal, something still beyond the reach of acoustic science. Because of its intimate relationship with human perception, the science of acoustics is still a field full of challenges and questions to explore. —LCK

"If Music Is the Architect . . ."
Edward Rothstein
New York Times, May 22, 2004

After Charles Garnier designed the Paris Opera in the 1870's, he called acoustics a "bizarre science."

"Nowhere did I find a positive rule to guide me," he wrote. "I must explain that I have adopted no principle, that my plan has been based on no theory, and that I leave success or failure to chance alone." He compared the acoustician to an acrobat "who closes his eyes and clings to the ropes of an ascending balloon."

The science of acoustics has taken flight since then, but not without many a deflated reputation and misguided journey along the way. Over the last 50 years, more computing power has been applied to acoustic data than ever before, but most big halls have turned out to be dry and pale frames for music.

After all, Avery Fisher Hall had been planned as the apotheosis of the new science of acoustics: Leo L. Beranek, its first acoustic designer, was an electrical engineer who studied signal processing and noise dampening. He had surveyed more than 50 concert halls throughout the world. Nonetheless, Fisher Hall, then named Philharmonic Hall, opened in 1962 to widespread unease. Fourteen years later, the inside was destroyed and replaced. But the problems didn't end, and so, after decades of tinkering, Lincoln Center announced this week that sometime after 2009, the hall would be gutted again.

Some of those problems, of course, are particular to Fisher Hall. Against Mr. Beranek's advice, for example, the hall's original volume and shape were altered to allow more seating. The acoustics in the latest version are also not as bad as their reputation: for instance, the hall's renowned glare became far more mellow once its resident orchestra, the New York Philharmonic, shed the brash nerviness it had cultivated in the 1980's.

But Fisher has also faced the problem of any hall that is less than great; it cannot compare to Carnegie Hall or to Symphony Hall in Boston or to the major halls of Vienna or Amsterdam, where every great orchestra has played and the luckiest listeners have sat: halls where sound can seem to have both substance and space, surrounding and, at times, caressing the listener. As Mr. Beranek himself wrote, "The old halls that are still standing are among the best that were built." That is why they are still standing.

The missteps in Fisher Hall, however, may also reflect a deeper confusion about the nature of concert halls and the role acoustics plays within them. This is an artistic issue, not a scientific one. For a great hall not only determines how music is heard, but also helps determine what music is written. Halls don't just present culture, they shape it.

As Michael Forsyth shows in his 1985 history of concert halls, "Buildings for Music: The Architect, the Musician and the Listener from the 17th Century to the Present Day" (M.I.T. Press), each style of music is associated with a style of space. Gregorian chant, with its measured pace and contrapuntal simplicity, seems inseparable from reverberant cathedrals and stone walls. The same spaces would muddle the harmonic transformations and abrupt motives of a Beethoven piano sonata. The gestural elegance of music for the Baroque court would be immediately lost in an outdoor amphitheater. Some of the gracious, expansive charm of Handel's organ concertos may derive from his awareness that they were being performed in the Rotunda of the Ranelagh Garden in London, where the listening public would promenade.

So, too, with the concert hall. It is no accident that its main repertory remains music that was specifically written to be played in such halls—symphonies, concertos, overtures—or that the music written during the 19th century, when concert halls moved to the center of musical life, remained the music at the center of concert hall life. The building is inseparable from its origins and from the music it inspired. Other musics visit the concert hall; they are not at home in it.

The building defines the nature of the listening public as well. When a concert hall's acoustics fail to welcome listeners into a world of felt sound, when they strip away resonance and emphasize distance and detail, they seem to alter the communal function of the concert hall. They make music seem as if it were something existing "out there," something to be respectfully and carefully heard rather than something intimately and urgently shared.

But that is what tended to happen to concert hall sound during much of the 20th century, and that, too, reflected a changing aesthetic. The music of Modernism demanded a kind of sonic ruthlessness, a crispness and unforgiving clarity. Often, it took a polemical stance toward the mainstream audience as well. How could this not affect the sonic character of halls?

This development also coincided with the beginnings of acoustics as a science. The first acoustical specialist ever to work on a concert hall was Wallace Clement Sabine, a physicist at Harvard University, who discovered important laws governing sonic reverberation and applied them to the design of Symphony Hall in Boston. That hall, which opened in 1900, now bears a plaque calling itself "the first auditorium in the world to be built in known conformity with acoustical laws."

But Symphony Hall was the last great concert hall of the 19th century rather than the first of the 20th. It was unaffected by Modernism. It had a single dedicated function: to serve orchestral sound. Sabine was trying to discover the nature of acoustic success, not reinvent it.

Afterward, as Emily Thompson shows in "The Soundscape of Modernity: Architectural Acoustics and the Culture of Listening in America, 1900–1933" (M.I.T. Press, 2002), acoustics took on a life of its own. The Acoustical Society of America was organized in 1929. Increasingly, electrical tools were used not just in analyzing sound but also in reproducing sound, both in the halls and the home. The sonic frame of reference shifted.

The grand movie palaces of the early decades of the century, for example, were meant to invoke European opera houses and had similar acoustics. (Some even featured orchestras to accompany silent films.) But by the late 1920's, speakers and amplification were essential for the new talkies. When Radio City Music Hall opened in 1932, its acoustics presumed amplification. As the concert hall became more clinical, the theater became more enveloping.

Ms. Thompson also argues that one of the main preoccupations of acousticians of the time was not the presentation of sound, but its prevention: sound control became an industry. The ability to control sound, either through dampening or amplification, also affected the evolution of concert halls. During the 1930's and 40's, Ms. Thompson points out, halls were often built with drastic dampening in the auditorium and increased reverberation on the stage: the hall began to resemble a loudspeaker.

Mr. Beranek described the effect of the Kleinhans Music Hall, built in 1940 in Buffalo, as "rather like listening to a very fine FM stereophonic reproducing system in a carpeted living room." The halls of the late 20th century have often been described as having a hi-fi sound. (In the case of Avery Fisher Hall, hi-fi was even the source of its main donor's fortune.)

In addition, the function of the hall itself began to change. Carnegie Hall has always been host to a wide variety of music, but its standard for design and sound was the orchestra. The premise of the late-20th-century hall was that while it created a home for an orchestra, it should be adaptable to all musical styles and functions.

So it has become customary to speak of "tuning a hall." Philharmonic Hall had adjustable panels; so does Avery Fisher. Many new halls go even further, with adjustable hollowed spaces and panels, variously called resonance chambers, clouds, canopies and closets. In some cases (like that of the New York State Theater when it is used by the New York City Opera), there are even electronically controlled sound-shaping speakers. Given psychoacoustical research into sound perception, and given the way ears are now accustomed to artificially hyped home theaters and electronically processed sound, who knows what temptations lie ahead?

This means that the hall is no longer a force that inspires particular styles of music and forms particular communities. It is instead meant to give way before their varied demands. It serves; it does not shape. So the hall has less of a focus. Instead of serving one ideal well—the ideal embodied in a 19th-century orchestral hall—it serves all ideals with compromise.

Is it possible that this makes it more difficult to love a new hall deeply, let alone to love deeply its sound? This may be why some of the most affecting musical spaces of the last decade have not been the large halls, but the smaller ones, built for specific purposes.

Perhaps the next Avery Fisher Hall will break with this tradition, and new forms of culture will emerge. But the risk is that it will be something of a hybrid: a throwback to the 19th century in its presence and ostensible function, a representative of the 20th in its requirements for clarity and demotic variability, and a harbinger of the 21st in that it will be so malleable that it will hardly matter when it finally gives way before yet another incarnation.

Computational Treatments of Waves

3

Reversing time seems like an impossibility, but when it refers to computer simulations of events, it becomes a useful tool. Any loud noise in an urban environment will be reflected and distorted by the complicated canyons of the buildings. A listener hears not just the direct sound but many reflections or echoes, which makes it nearly impossible to pinpoint the source of the sound. Sometimes that might be a nuisance, such as when trying to locate the source of a siren, or it might be a critical problem, such as when the police or military are trying to locate a sniper.

This article by the U.S. Army's Cold Regions Research and Engineering Laboratory's Donald G. Albert and Lanbo Liu, who is also with the University of Connecticut, shows how collecting the acoustic signal from a gunshot in a full-scale model village and then reversing the timing of the signals using a computer can pinpoint the location of the gun. —LCK

From "A Shot in the City: Locating a Sound Source in an Urban Environment"
by Lanbo Liu and Donald G. Albert
Paper presented at the 147th Acoustical Society
of America Meeting, New York, NY, May 28, 2001

Sound propagation in an urban environment is complicated by the presence of buildings. The sound waves
reflect from building walls and diffract (or bend) around
corners. Because of the many diffractions and echoes, it
is difficult for a listener to locate the source of the sound
waves, especially when the source is not directly visible.
(Where is that ambulance siren coming from?)

At the last Acoustical Society of America Meeting,
we discussed measurements of these effects made in an
artificial urban setting (a full scale model village used
for training) and a method of mathematically simulating
these sounds on a PC. In this paper, we apply a technique called time reversal processing to locate sound
sources in urban areas. This method has been previously
used in medical imaging and treatment, underwater
communication, and other applications, and a short
course on this method was taught at the last ASA
Meeting by ASA Fellows Mathias Fink and William
Kuperman. We are applying it to urban sound propagation for the first time.

How does it work? In the time reversal method, a
network of simple, low-resolution sensors in the
urban area detects sound waves. These signals are
complicated, since they include all the many echoes
and other arrivals from the wave "bouncing" around

amongst the buildings. We then turn completely to a computer. It receives the sound signals from the sensors, and we use it to generate a backwards version of the detected sound waves. Then, using a model of sound propagation in the urban area, we rebroadcast the sound waves in a virtual urban environment. The waves eventually return and focus at the original source point, enabling us to pinpoint the location of a sound, such as an explosion or gunshot! By having a few microphones somewhere in the village, we can use the computer model and the time reversal technique to locate the sound source.

By measuring the sound at a few locations in the village and using the computer model to propagate them back from the receiver locations, a focus of sound energy occurs at the original source location.

. . . The sound waves emanate from the various speakers, bounce off of the buildings, and concentrate ([dark blob, bottom image on page 48]) at the approximate source of the original shot, (["X" in the top image on page 48]). This model run shows that the correct source location is found from just a few sensors, all of them being shielded from the view of the source location. With further development this method has the potential of improving sound source (sniper) detection and other sensor systems.

In the ASA short course, Drs. Fink and Kuperman showed that time-reversal procedure also works if you physically rebroadcast the sounds into the actual environment, such as an underwater minefield, or a kidney-stone patient's body. They gave many examples

Forward: Sound from the shot

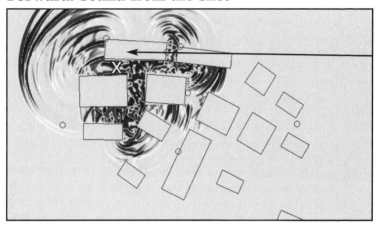

Computer simulation showing sound waves from a shot (the black "**X**") bouncing off buildings in the village.

Reverse: Locating the shot

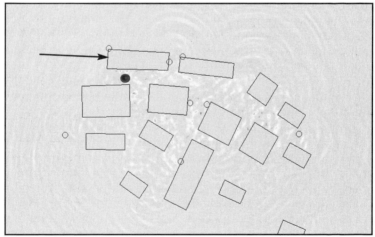

The result of modeling the sounds using the Time Reversal Method. Notice the concentration of sound waves [dark blob] indicating the source location of the original shot sound.

of applications in the medical, communication, and signal processing fields.

The Doppler shift (also called the Doppler effect) in the frequency of a wave being emitted by a moving source is familiar to most people. For example, most of us have noticed that an approaching siren sound is higher in pitch than a receding siren. In this mathematically advanced article, N. Seddon and T. Bearpark, both of the Advanced Technology Centre in Bristol, England, report on experimental observations of the inverse Doppler shift, which does the opposite. In the inverse Doppler shift, waves emitted by approaching sources are lower in frequency, while waves emitted by a receding source are shifted to higher frequencies. The ordinary Doppler shift has found many applications in radar and medicine, for example, and the inverse Doppler effect may likewise have as yet unexplored applications.

This report mentions in passing some advanced concepts in wave propagation, such as dispersion (when waves of different wavelengths travel at different speeds), but it relies on an understanding of group velocity (the speed at which a collection of wave crests

travel) and phase velocity (the speed at which an individual wave crest travels). —LCK

From "Observation of the Inverse Doppler Effect"
by N. Seddon and T. Bearpark
Science, November 28, 2003

The Doppler effect is the well-known phenomenon by which the frequency of a wave is shifted according to the relative velocity of the source and the observer (*1, 2*). Our conventional understanding of the Doppler effect, from the schoolroom to everyday experience of passing vehicles, is that increased frequencies are measured when a source and observer approach each other. Applications of the effect are widely established and include radar, laser vibrometry, bloodflow measurement, and the search for new astronomical objects. The inverse Doppler effect refers to frequency shifts that are in the opposite sense to those described above; for example, increased frequencies would be measured on reflection of waves from a receding boundary. Demonstration of this counterintuitive phenomenon requires a fundamental change in the way that radiation is reflected from a moving boundary, and, despite a wide range of theoretical work that spans the past 60 years, the effect has not previously been verified experimentally.

Although inverse Doppler shifts have been predicted to occur in particular dispersive media (*3–8*) and in the near zone of three-dimensional dipoles (*9–11*), these schemes are difficult to implement experimentally and have not yet been realized. However, recent advances in the design of composite condensed media (metamaterials) offers new and exciting possibilities for the control of radiation. In particular, materials with a negative refractive index (NRI) (*12–14*) and the use of shock discontinuities in photonic crystals (*15*) and transmission lines (*16, 17*) have been proposed to show inverse Doppler shifts.

Conventional Doppler shifts occur on reflection of waves propagating in media with normal dispersion from a moving boundary (Fig. 1A). Inverse Doppler shifts are predicted to occur on reflection of waves propagating in media with anomalous dispersion from a moving boundary (Fig. 1B). The essential difference is that waves in normally dispersive media have group velocity, ν_g, and phase velocity, ν_p, that are parallel ($\nu_g \cdot \nu_p > 0$), whereas waves in anomalously dispersive media have ν_g and ν_p that are antiparallel ($\nu_g \cdot \nu_p < 0$). For a wave in a normal medium ($\nu_g \cdot \nu_p > 0$) of frequency ω_i in a stationary frame of reference incident on a receding boundary, the boundary velocity and the phase velocity of the incident wave are parallel; therefore, the incident field in the frame of the receding boundary oscillates with a relatively low frequency. Boundary conditions in this case dictate that the frequency of the reflected wave is less than ω_i, as expected for the conventional Doppler effect (Fig. 1A). In the anomalously dispersive medium, the phase velocity of the incident wave and the boundary velocity are antiparallel (Fig. 1B). In this case, the incident field in the frame of the boundary oscillates with a relatively

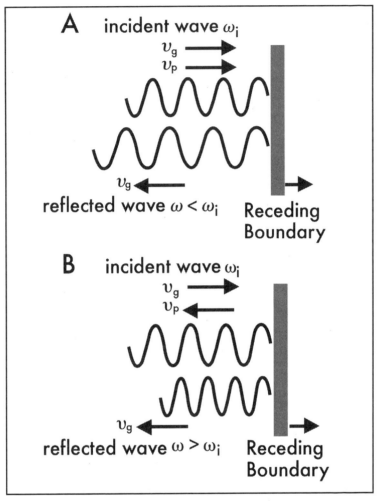

Fig. 1. Reflection of waves from a receding boundary. **(A)** A wave propagating in a medium with normal dispersion with frequency ω_i, phase velocity ν_p, and group velocity ν_g in a stationary frame of reference is incident on a receding boundary, resulting in a conventional Doppler shift. **(B)** A wave propagating in a medium with anomalous dispersion with frequency ω_i, phase velocity ν_p, and group velocity ν_g in a stationary frame of reference is incident on the boundary, resulting in an inverse Doppler shift.

high frequency, and boundary conditions dictate that the frequency of the reflected wave is greater than ω_i, as expected for the inverse Doppler effect.

We have realized experimentally the situation illustrated in Fig. 1B by reflecting waves from a moving discontinuity in an electrical transmission line . . .

Conclusive observation of inverse Doppler shifts has its basis in agreement between predictions from the Doppler equation, a numerical model of the transmission line, and experimental measurements. The absolute velocity of waves in the transmission line was typically $c/15$ (where c is the speed of light in free space) and the nonrelativistic Doppler equation

$$\frac{\omega_r}{\omega_i} = \frac{1 - (\vec{\nu_s} \cdot \vec{\nu_i})/\nu_i^2}{1 - (\nu_s \cdot \nu_r)/\nu_r^2}$$

was used to predict the frequencies of Doppler-shifted waves. Here, ν_s, ν_i, ν_r, ω_i, ω_r are the shock propagation velocity, incident wave phase velocity, reflected wave phase velocity, frequency of the incident wave, and frequency of the reflected wave, respectively . . .

In the experiment, pump pulses were injected into the line, and, with the use of a dc bias current to set the initial condition of the nonlinear components, the velocity of the shock discontinuity and consequently the phase velocity of wave were varied. The discontinuity velocity was reduced sufficiently to produce waves with phase velocity $0.25\nu_o < \nu_p < 0.35\nu_o$ . . . and RF signals were monitored between the input terminals of the transmission line and the propagating discontinuity (*19*).

Data from the numerical simulation, the experiment, and the Doppler shift calculation are shown in Fig. 4. The agreement between these sets of data is clear and gives a high degree of confidence that the higher frequency signal in each case is produced by the inverse Doppler effect.

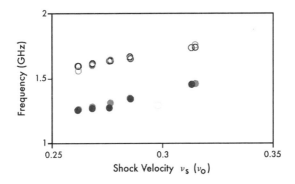

Fig. 4. Data from the experiment, the numerical model, and the Doppler equation. Solid [gray] circles represent the lower frequency experimental signal. Solid [black] circles represent the lower frequency numerically simulated signal. Open [gray] circles represent the experimentally measured Doppler signal. Open [black] circles represent the Doppler signal from the numerical model. Open [black] circles represent the signals predicted by the Doppler equation.

The technique described here produces frequency shifts of over 20% from a single Doppler reflection by creating a boundary that has a similar velocity to the phase velocity of the incident wave. This shift is over five orders of magnitude greater than Doppler shifts from solid objects moving with kinematic velocities. Frequency shifts of 100 % or more should be attainable by designing the underlying dispersion characteristics appropriately. Reflection of waves from electromagnetic shock discontinuities offers the opportunity to produce radiation sources that are tunable over a wide range and capable of simultaneously generating several frequency components that are not harmonically related. The technique is also applicable to systems with electronic nonlinearity that operate in the 100-GHz region (*26*) and may form the basis for tunable sources of terahertz radiation and other frequency regions that are difficult to access. However, the principle point of this report is a demonstration that it is possible to fundamentally change the interaction of radiation with a moving boundary and to produce inverse Doppler shifts.

References and Notes

1. C. Doppler, *Abh. Koniglichen Bohmischen Ges. Wiss.* 2, 465 (1843).
2. C. H. Papas, *Theory of Electromagnetic Wave Propagation* (McGraw-Hill, New York, 1965).
3. I. Frank, *J. Phys. USSR* 7, 49 (1943).
4. K. S. H. Lee, *Radio Sci.* 3, 1098 (1968).
5. M. Yu. Sorokin, *Radiophys. Quantum Elect.* 36, 410 (1993).
6. K. S. H. Lee, C. H. Papas, *J. Math. Phys.* 42, 189 (1963)
7. K. A. Barsukov, *Sov. Phys. Tech. Phys.* 7, 112 (1962).
8. K. A. Barsukov, A. A. Kolomenskii, *Sov. Phys. Tech. Phys.* 4, 868 (1959).
9. N. Engheta, A. R. Mikelson, C. H. Papas, *IEEE Trans. Antennas Propag.* AP-28, 512 (1980).
10. N. Engheta, *Recent Advances in Electromagnetic Theory* (Springer-Verlag, New York, 1990).
11. Y. Ben-Shimol, D. Censor, *Radio Sci.* 33, 463 (1998).
12. V. G. Veslago, *Sov. Phys. Usp.* 10, 509 (1968).
13. D. R. Smith, W. J. Padilla, D. C. Vier, S. C. Nemat-Nasser, S. Schultz, *Phys. Rev. Lett.* 84, 4184 (2000).
14. J. B. Pendry, *Phys. Rev. Lett.* 85, 3966 (2000).

15. E. J. Reed, M. Soljacic, J. D. Joannopoulos, *Phys. Rev Lett.* 91, 133901 (2003).
16. A. M. Belyantsev, A. B. Kozyrev, *Sov. Phys. Tech. Phys.* 45, 747 (2000).
17. A. M. Belyantsev, A. B. Kozyrev, *Sov. Phys. Tech. Phys.* 47, 1477 (2002).
19. Materials and methods are available as supporting material on *Science Online.*
26. A. M. Belyantsev, A. B. Kozyrev, *Int. J. Infrared Millimeter Waves* 19, 1571 (1998).

Excerpted with permission from Seddon, Nigel, and T. Bearpark, "Observation of the Inverse Doppler Effect," *Science* 302:1537–1540 (2003). © 2003 AAAS.

Not all waves are composed of steady, periodic waves. In fact, most of the waves encountered in the real world of science and engineering are aperiodic, noisy, intermittent, or transient. Traditional methods, which include long-standing Fourier analysis techniques, are not capable of extracting much of the information that lies hidden in such waves.

Paul Addison, professor of engineering at Napier University in Scotland and cofounder of CardioDigital Limited, has found that using "wavelets" in his analysis of the noisy signals extracted from the breathing patterns of newborn babies, for example, is a highly productive method of analysis. Wavelets are what their name suggests—small, wavelike functions that come in all shapes and sizes. By mathematically comparing the shape of the wavelet with different portions of the signal under analysis, very high-resolution temporal (time-varying) and spectral (frequency content) analysis of the signal can be performed. Professor Addison writes an enthusiastic exposition of this new way of looking at complicated wave data. —LCK

From "The Little Wave with the Big Future"
by Paul Addison
Physics World, **March 2004**

Eureka moments are so rare in science that when you have one, you don't forget it in a hurry. My colleagues and I at Napier University in Edinburgh were fortunate enough to have one such moment a few years ago when we were studying the signals from a medical device called a pulse oximeter. Widely used in hospitals to measure the percentage of blood haemoglobin that is saturated with oxygen, the device also provides an accurate measure of a patient's heart rate.

We had been trying to use the oximeter to measure how ill patients were, based on subtle changes to these signals, which repeat regularly once every heartbeat. Using the relatively new technique of "wavelet transforms," we suddenly realized that some of the regular patterns that were appearing in our signal were not caused by the beating heart. They were, in fact, caused by the patient's breathing. Moreover, the breathing signals were much clearer than could be measured using traditional methods. We have since used this technique to study the breathing patterns of newborn babies.

This finding, which I shall return to later, is one example of the many ways in which data can be analysed using wavelet transforms. The technique is ideal for teasing out information from signals that are aperiodic, noisy, intermittent or transient. It has been used by many different researchers to study climate patterns and financial indices, to monitor heartbeats and rotating machinery, to de-noise seismic signals and astronomical images, to characterize cracks and turbulence, and to compress electronic and medical images.

Many of the ideas behind wavelet transforms have been around for a long time. Indeed, the first "wavelet"—a simple, square waveform—was developed by the mathematician Alfred Haar at the beginning of the last century. But it was not until the mid-1980s that true wavelet-transform analysis was developed by Jean Morlet and Alex Grossmann. Morlet, who was an engineer with the French oil firm Elf Aquitane, developed the technique to study seismic signals. He then teamed up with Grossmann, who worked at the CNRS Centre for Theoretical Physics in Marseille, to formalize the mathematics of the wavelet transform.

Despite their efforts, wavelet analysis initially remained confined to a small, mainly mathematical, community with only a handful of scientific papers being published each year. At the end of the 1980s, however, two further important mathematical advances were made by Ingrid Daubechies at the Courant Institute in New York and by Stéphanie Mallat at the University of Pennsylvania. By the start of the 1990s, the stage was set for the practical application of wavelet analysis in science and engineering. As more and more researchers spotted the potential of the technique, a flurry of papers began to appear. That flurry has since turned into a blizzard, with over 1000 peer-reviewed papers now appearing each year.

Wavelet Basics

Wavelet analysis has some similarities with traditional Fourier analysis, which involves representing a signal as the sum of sines and cosines of various frequencies. A simple, square-wave signal with a magnitude $\pm a$, for example, is roughly equivalent to a series of cosines of increasing frequency: $a(\cos x) + a/3[\cos(x/3)] + a/5[\cos(x/5)] + \ldots$. Fourier analysis is particularly useful for gleaning the pertinent spectral characteristics in signals that do not change with time. It is also good at identifying the spectral components in relatively noisy signals that change in a regular fashion with time, such as the emission of radio waves from rotating neutron stars (pulsars). What Fourier analysis is not so good at, however, is investigating more complex, "non-stationary" signals, such as our heartbeat, where the component frequencies change with time. This is because it averages the key features of a time-varying signal of the entire length of the signal, which means that fine detail is lost.

In 1946 the Hungarian-born physicist Dennis Gabor—who later won the 1971 Nobel Prize for Physics by inventing holography—found a way of getting around this problem. While working for the firm Thomson-Houston in Rugby, UK, Gabor realized that the answer was to perform a Fourier analysis of only a small segment of the signal at a time. Moving incrementally along the signal provides a series of spectral analyses, each of which is located at a particular point

in time. But there is still a drawback with this "short-time Fourier transform" technique: it uses a window of fixed width. It therefore averages short-duration components and cannot capture those components that last longer than the window itself.

This is where wavelet analysis shines: it is able to take into account the scale of signal components. Wavelets are small, wave-like functions that come in all shapes and sizes [see figure 1a on page 61]. Some are smooth and look like a Mexican hat. Some are sharp functions with square edges. Others can be highly oscillatory, fractal or even complex. Wavelets are used to transform the signal under investigation into another representation that presents the signal information in a more useful form. Mathematically speaking, the wavelet transform is a convolution of the wavelet function with the signal (figure 1b). If the wavelet matches the shape of the signal well at a specific scale and location, then a large value of the transform is obtained. If, however, the wavelet and the signal do not correlate well then the transform value is small.

The choice of wavelet depends on the type of signal that is being investigated. Short-duration (high-frequency) features are best interrogated using narrow wavelets, while longer-lasting (low-frequency) features are more suited to wider wavelets. Changing the type of wavelet lets one zoom in on individual small-scale, high-frequency components or pan out to pick up larger-scale, low-frequency components (figure 1c). In practice the transform is computed at a series of points in time along the signal and for different sizes (i.e. frequencies)

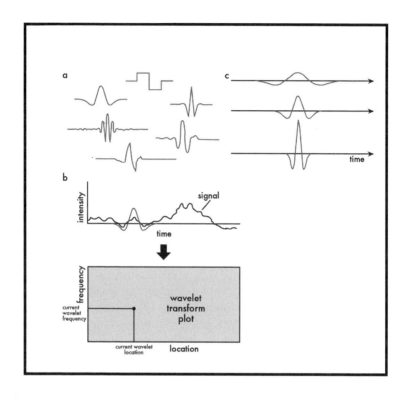

Figure 1. (*a*) Wavelets are used to transform a signal into another representation that presents the information in a more useful form. A few common examples of wavelets are shown here, including the square "Haar" wavelet. (*b*) In the wavelet-analysis technique the wavelet function [gray] is "convoluted with the signal [black]. If the wavelet matches the signal well, a large number is obtained. If the wavelength matches the signal poorly, a low number is obtained. The transform is computed at different times in the signal, with wavelets of different frequency used on each occasion. The transform value for each position and frequency of the wavelet function are usually plotted on a 2D plane. (*c*) Stretching and squeezing the wavelet during the transform process changes its frequency make up. The height of the wavelet also changes to conserve its signal energy.

of wavelet at each point. The values of the transform at every time and frequency can then be plotted on a 2D "transform plane," with time down one axis and frequency along the other.

Wavelet Transforms in Practice

In my research, a three-minute signal will typically be transformed at 10,000 separate points in time using wavelets of 200 different sizes. The resulting two million transform points can be computed relatively quickly using a standard desktop PC with software such as Matlab or Mathcad. For real-time applications the wavelet transform is usually updated live. If complex wavelets—containing both a real and imaginary component—are used, both the phase and the modulus of the transform value can be used to study the signal. A time-frequency plot with energy density on the third axis—the wavelet scalogram—can then be obtained from the square of the modulus.

The exact number of transform points depends on how the transform has been calculated. If it is computed only at selected locations on the signal and for a restricted range of scales—so-called discrete wavelet transforms—the resolution is very poor. But if the transform is computed over a continuous range of wavelet scales and signal locations—so-called continuous wavelet transforms—the resolution can be significantly improved.

The advantage of the discrete approach is that it is faster because it uses a cunning piece of mathematical jiggery-pokery called "multi-resolution analysis." Formulated by Mallat while he was a graduate student at Pennsylvania in the late 1980s, it allows the wavelet transform to be calculated very quickly using a set of wavelets that are "orthogonal" to each other. In other words, the wavelet functions would have zero output if convolved with themselves.

The resulting discrete wavelet transform (DWT) is both "complete" and has "zero redundancy," which means that all the signal information is contained in the resulting transform and none is duplicated between transform coefficients. By converting the signal into its DWT coefficients and then removing all except those containing the most pertinent signal information, the resulting transform is much smaller in size, which provides a good way of compressing a signal. Performing an "inverse transform" on the remaining components recreates a signal that very nearly matches the original. This is the basis of image-compression algorithms such as those used by the new JPEG2000 format. Developed by the Joint Photographic Experts Group, it creates a file that is much smaller than—but looks similar to—the original.

Watermarks, Water Wakes and Watercolours

Discrete wavelet transforms are ideal for analysing image files and other data sets that contain two or more dimensions because they can be rapidly calculated using multi-resolution analysis and because there are relatively few resulting transform coefficients. One application is in "digital watermarking," which protects the owners of digital multimedia objects against unauthorized copyright infringement. The technique involves adding information that is imperceptible to the human eye to a digital multimedia object. This added information can then be used to check if the object has been unlawfully copied at a later stage.

Many researchers—both in universities and industry—are now trying to incorporate wavelet transforms into the watermarking process by hiding secret information in the transform coefficients. When the inverse transform is calculated, the reconstructed image appears the same to the human eye, although not to a machine that can detect the watermark. Watermarking is still an evolving science; researchers are, for example, trying to find out if the watermarked image can retain its security features even if it has been blurred, rotated, added to or otherwise altered . . .

Baby Breathing

In my own application of wavelet transforms, my colleagues and I have been developing methods to detect the very subtle respiration signals obtained through a patient's fingertip using a pulse oximeter. Based on the different ways in which oxygenated and deoxygenated haemoglobin absorb light, the device provides an accurate measure of not only blood-oxygen levels but also heart rate. It is widely used to monitor patients who are at risk of hypoxia—blood with too little oxygen—and can be found on any hospital ward.

The device is basically a box of electronic gadgetry that includes a display connected to a light probe. The probe is attached to the patient's body, usually the finger.

Red and infrared light is then shone sequentially through the body tissue via a fast-switching light-emitting diode circuit. The transmitted light is picked up by a suitably positioned photodiode. The resulting signal repeats its waveform every time the heart beats.

We found that wavelet transforms—in the form of a complex sinusoidal function within a Gaussian window—were good at finding faint perturbations in the signal caused by the patient's breathing. In fact, we found that some of the regular patterns in the transform plots were too long to have been caused by the beating heart. It was then that the penny dropped. Our method was, in fact, picking up the rhythm of the patient's breathing—and was doing so with much more clarity than could be achieved using traditional methods . . .

Watch This Wavelet Space

I remember attending a Royal Society conference on wavelet transforms in 1999, when an eminent professor, whom I would rather not name, was asked if the technique would ever replace Fourier analysis. "I wouldn't like to say that wavelet analysis will supersede Fourier analysis," he replied, "but rather that Fourier methods will gradually become marginalized." Certainly the academic literature—and, perhaps more tellingly, the patent literature—is now full of wavelet-based time-frequency techniques, many of which supersede traditional Fourier spectral methods.

But if the professor's prediction is ever to come true, a wide-spread and deep-rooted Fourier mentality needs to be overcome. The challenge now is for researchers to appreciate the advantages of wavelet transforms over other time-frequency techniques. It would be great if wavelet transforms were taught to all physics and engineering undergraduates, but I am not holding my breath. Such a change will probably be driven by calls from industry once the new techniques have become widely used in the commercial world.

It is, however, going to take quite a few years yet for the dust to settle in wavelet space. When it does—and the merits of the new wavelet-based analysis methods become more obvious—I believe that the wavelet transform, in all its forms, will become the time-frequency analysis tool of choice. By allowing signal features and the frequency of their occurrence to be determined simultaneously, the wavelet transforms have a lot to offer the scientific community. The little wave, I have no doubt, has a big future.

Reprinted with permission from *Physics World*.

The story of sonoluminescence is a fascinating tale of the scientific method in action. At the start, a team of respected scientists make exciting and hopeful claims that they had created a clean energy source, fusion, on their desktop. But the claim is proven incorrect through the relentless examination of peer review; other scientists following up with their own experiments could not reproduce their results. In the first article excerpt, writer Hazel Muir reports on the claims that sonoluminescence, the flash of light observed inside tiny bubbles exposed to strong sound waves, was caused by the fusion of two deuterium atoms—hydrogen with a neutron. If it had been found to be true, it would have been one of the most important discoveries in science in recent years, making an energy source like that of a small sun available to humankind.

But this was not the case. In the second article excerpt, physicist Detlef Lohse, from the University of Twente in the Netherlands, *describes how sonoluminescence—gas bubbles collapsing under the influence of powerful acoustic waves—can be viewed as "a high-temperature, high-pressure miniature reactor," offering a controlled environment for high-temperature reaction rate measurements. —LCK*

"Bursting with Energy"
by Hazel Muir
New Scientist, March 9, 2002

Will popping a few bubbles solve the world's power problems?

Nuclear fusion can be achieved by popping bubbles in nail polish remover, claims a team led by Rusi Taleyarkhan at Oak Ridge National Laboratory in Tennessee.

"If it is true, it is truly amazing," says Andrea Prosperetti, who studies bubbles at Johns Hopkins University in Baltimore. For starters, it would allow physicists to study fusion on their bench tops, although this is already possible with low-power accelerators. More tantalising, but even more controversial, is the prospect of harnessing this form of fusion to produce clean energy.

Bubble fusion is already provoking comparisons with the cold fusion fiasco in 1989, when Martin Fleischmann of Southampton University and Stanley Pons of the University of Utah announced that they had triggered nuclear fusion at room temperature by electrolysing heavy water. Others failed to replicate their results.

The first attempt to duplicate Taleyarkhan's results has also failed. "Our experiment saw no evidence for nuclear fusion," says Mike Saltmarsh, a member of another team at Oak Ridge that tried the experiment again with a more sophisticated detection system. "This does not prove that no nuclear fusion is going on," Saltmarsh points out. But if any fusion is occurring, it must be at a very low level.

Nevertheless, Taleyarkhan's results are being taken more seriously than Fleischmann and Pons's. For one thing, they appear in a prestigious journal. More importantly, there's nothing cold about this fusion. Collapsing bubbles really might approach the temperatures needed for fusion.

Getting energy from nuclear fusion has been the goal of many scientists. One way is to fuse two deuterium atoms—hydrogen with a neutron. This reaction yields lots of energy and creates either inert helium and free neutrons, or hydrogen and radioactive tritium—hydrogen with two neutrons. Tritium has a half-life of just 12 years and can be turned into helium by fusing it with more deuterium. So unlike existing fission reactors, fusion wouldn't produce mountains of radioactive waste.

The catch is that to overcome the repulsion between deuterium nuclei, they have to be heated to around 10 million degrees Celsius, the temperature in the heart of the Sun. Containing matter at such extraordinary temperatures is extremely difficult. No one has developed a fusion reactor that generates more energy than it uses up.

It's been speculated that collapsing bubbles could be an alternative to giant reactors. For decades it has been known that sound waves in water can generate tiny bubbles that heat to thousands of degrees and emit light as they collapse—a phenomenon called sonoluminescence. If these bubbles get near the magic 10 million degrees, nuclear fusion might occur.

Taleyarkhan's team thought it might be possible to achieve such temperatures in acetone, or nail varnish remover. To achieve fusion, they replaced the hydrogen atoms in the acetone with deuterium and chilled the liquid to $0\,^{\circ}C$. Blasting it with a neutron beam generated tiny bubbles. Sound waves then expanded the bubbles to about 2 millimetres before they imploded.

The team reports detecting emissions of high-energy neutrons that coincided with light and shock waves from the imploding bubbles. The neutrons had energies of 2.5 million electronvolts, which is what you'd expect for neutrons released as deuterium fuses to form helium. They also detected raised levels of tritium. No evidence of fusion was detected when normal acetone was used instead.

But many scientists doubt that fusion took place. In theory, collapsing bubbles could reach astronomical temperatures if they remain perfectly spherical as they implode. But real-life bubbles don't usually behave this way. The actual temperatures in the collapsing bubbles are probably more like 10,000 or 20,000 degrees, Prosperetti says. "From this to the millions you need for fusion is quite a stretch."

All the experts are now keen to see more attempts to repeat the experiment. But even if these show that fusion does occur, there's no evidence that the process could generate more energy than it devours. Of course, it is possible that some clever technology might eventually squeeze enough energy out of the bubbles. "I wouldn't rule it out," Prosperetti says. "But this field has seen some weird claims in the past. Lots of people have ended up with mud on their faces."

Reprinted with permission from *New Scientist*.

"Sonoluminescence: Inside a Micro-Reactor"
by Detlef Lohse
Nature, July 25, 2002

Gas bubbles in a liquid can convert sound energy into light. Detailed measurements of a single bubble show that, in fact, most of the sound energy goes into chemical reactions taking place inside this "micro-reactor."

"Single-bubble sonoluminescence" is the remarkable phenomenon that describes how a gas bubble in liquid, exposed to a strong, standing sound wave, collapses and emits light. First observed 12 years ago,[1] the basic physics of the process seems to be understood.[2] That there is strong and crucial chemical activity inside the sonoluminescing bubble had already been hypothesized[3] and indirectly confirmed.[4, 5] Now Didenko and Suslick[6] . . .

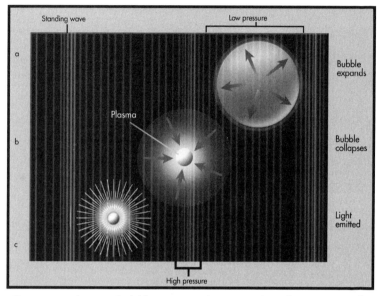

Figure 1 Glowing bubbles: a sound wave in liquid causes sonoluminescence. **a,** At low pressure, a gas bubble expands dramatically, until **b,** an increase in sound-wave pressure triggers its collapse. As the temperature inside the bubble soars to over 10,000 K, the gas becomes partly ionized, forming a plasma. Finally, **c,** recombination of electrons and ions results in light emission. But according to Didenko and Suslick,[6] more energy goes into chemical reactions in the bubble gas than is released as light.

have performed the first direct measurements of the reaction rates inside an individual bubble as it sonoluminesces. Energy-wise, it seems that a sonoluminescing bubble should be viewed not as a light bulb, but rather as a high-temperature, high-pressure, miniature reactor.

The process of sonoluminescence is shown in Fig. 1. First, at low sound pressure, the micrometre-size bubble expands, increasing its volume by a factor of 1,000. When the pressure increases again, the bubble eventually collapses dramatically, shrinking to a radius that corresponds to solid-state densities. The compression drives up the temperature of the gas inside the bubble—through this "adiabatic" heating the bubble interior is thought to reach around 10,000–20,000 K. Consequently, the gas becomes partly ionized and the recombination of electrons and ions leads to the emission of light.

As the bubble expands, gas dissolved in the liquid enters the bubble. At the point of adiabatic collapse, some of these gases are trapped inside the hot bubble and start to react. For example, nitrogen molecules dissociate into nitrogen radicals and then react to form gases such as NH and NO. These highly soluble gases re-dissolve in the surrounding water when the bubble cools down. As the bubble expansion begins again, the next reaction cycle starts. Didenko and Suslick's calculations of the energy budget of sonoluminescence show that the amount of energy going into endothermic chemical reactions inside the bubble is two orders of magnitude higher than that going into light emission.

However, one complication that still remains is that the temperature inside the bubble cannot be measured directly. It has to be deduced either from the bubble dynamics (for example, by Mie scattering[1, 7, 8]) or from the properties of the light emitted (spectral information, intensity and widths of the light pulses[9]). Either way, assumptions have to be made, whether in the modelling of the bubble dynamics[10] and the thermodynamics of the heat and mass exchange between the bubble and its surroundings, or in the modelling of the plasma physical processes to predict the observable light properties.

The information obtained in these two ways should obviously be consistent in a viable theory of sonoluminescence. Even then, we can't be certain, as errors arising in the modelling of the bubble interior and light emission could compensate for each other. But Didenko and Suslick's measurements of the chemical reaction rates open up a third experimental window on the process. This extra constraint reduces the freedom in modelling, leading towards further convergence of the models.

It is astounding how many sub-disciplines of physics and chemistry have played a role in disentangling what happens in single-bubble sonoluminescence. They range from acoustics, fluid dynamics, plasma physics, thermodynamics, atomic physics and spectroscopy, to physical and analytical chemistry, chemical kinetics, dynamical-system theory and applied mathematics in general. But nuclear and fusion physics are not on the list: the final conclusion from Didenko and Suslick's results is that it is the chemical reaction rate within the bubble that limits the efficiency of bubble collapse. So "bubble fusion"—an energy-generating fusion reaction in the high-density, high-temperature interior of the collapsing bubble[11]—is most unlikely.

Although fusion may be out of reach, there are other uses for sonoluminescent bubbles. The extreme conditions inside the bubble are adjustable through external parameters such as forcing pressure or water temperature, so the bubble can be considered as a controlled high-temperature reaction chamber, offering opportunities to measure reaction rates in extreme temperature and pressure regimes. But understanding single bubbles is not enough. Before this knowledge can be applied to sonochemistry[12]—the enhancement of chemical reactions through ultrasound in a bubbly fluid—a better understanding of bubble-bubble interactions will be needed.

Just as the hydrogen atom was the basic model for larger atoms and molecules, so the single bubble is the simplest building block in the physics of a sound-driven bubbly fluid. With the detailed understanding of the hydrogen atom, atomic physics began to flourish. By analogy, now that there is a basic understanding of single-bubble sonoluminescence and the chemical activity inside the bubble, I expect also a flourishing of cavitation physics.

References

1. Gaitan, D. F. An Experimental Investigation of Acoustic Cavitation in Gaseous Liquids. Thesis, Univ. Mississippi (1990).
2. Brenner, M. P., Hilgenfeldt, S. & Lohse, D. *Rev. Mod. Phys.* 74, 425–484 (2002).
3. Lohse, D., Brenner, M. P., Dupont, T. F., Hilgenfeldt, S. & Johnston, B. *Phys. Rev. Lett.* 78, 1359–1362 (1997).
4. Matula, T. J. & Crum, L. A. *Phys. Rev. Lett.* 80, 865-868 (1998).
5. Ketterling, J. A. & Apfel, R. E. *Phys. Rev. Lett.* 81, 4991–4994 (1998).
6. Didenko, Y. T. & Suslick, K. S. *Nature* 418, 394–397 (2002).
7. Weninger, K. R., Barber, B. P. & Putterman, S. J. *Phys. Rev. Lett.* 78, 1799–1802 (1997).
8. Matula, T. J. Phil. *Trans. R. Soc. Lond.* A 357, 225–249 (1999).
9. Gompf, B., Gunther, R., Nick, G., Pecha, R. & Eisenmenger, W. *Phys. Rev. Lett.* 79, 1405–1408 (1997).
10. Plesset, M. S. & Prosperetti, A. *Annu. Rev. Fluid Mech.* 9, 145–185 (1977).
11. Taleyarkhan, R. P. et al. *Science* 295, 1868–1873 (2002).
12. Suslick, K. S. *Science* 247, 1439–1445 (1990).

Reprinted with permission from the Nature Publishing Group.

Infrasound is a silent sound wave at a frequency below 20 Hz, too low for human ears to hear. This doesn't mean that infrasound is unimportant; it still is felt by humans, invoking emotional responses such as those felt when listening to church music in a cathedral. It is also used by many animals to communicate, and it is emitted by a plethora of natural phenomena, including volcanoes, earthquakes, and avalanches. Human activity, such as nuclear testing, also creates infrasound. Since infrasound can come from so many different sources, science writer Kate Ramsayer interviewed National Aeronautics and Space Administration (NASA) scientists, an acoustician, geophysicists, an oceanographer, and biologists to find out how infrasound is used and detected by scientists in a wide range of fields. —LCK

"Infrasonic Symphony: The Greatest Sounds Never Heard"
by Kate Ramsayer
Science News, January 10, 2004

"Let me start off with a riddle," says NASA scientist Allan J. Zuckerwar. In his office in Hampton, Va., he rattles off items as dissimilar as rhinoceroses, supersonic aircraft, and hurricanes. "Now, what do they have in common?" The answer, Zuckerwar explains, is that each one generates silent infrasound—long sound waves at a frequency below 20 hertz. People can't hear anything below that frequency, probably for good reason.

Otherwise, they'd be bombarded by the constant din of wind, the intermittent groaning of Earth, and the occasional distant explosion. But scientists are eavesdropping on volcanoes, avalanches, earthquakes, and meteorites to discern these phenomena's infrasound signatures and see what new information infrasound might reveal.

Just as seismic waves travel through Earth, infrasonic waves travel through the air. And the lower the frequency of the waves, the farther they can travel without losing strength. Scientists first detected infrasound in 1883, when the eruption of the Krakatoa volcano in Indonesia sent inaudible sound waves careening around the world, affecting barometric readings.

Infrasonic research gained significant attention and funding in the 1950s, when the United States and the Soviet Union used infrasound to detect each other's atmospheric nuclear testing. Interest declined when aboveground bomb testing was banned in 1963 as part of the Limited Test Ban Treaty.

But lately, scientists have turned back to infrasound, in large part because of the Comprehensive Test Ban Treaty, which was adopted by the United Nations in 1996. The monitoring section in this treaty calls for a global network of 60 infrasound-detecting stations to search for treaty violations.

Each of the 24 monitoring stations established to date consists of an array of specialized infrasonic microphones that can detect the strength of a sound, its frequency, and the direction from which it's coming. The monitoring stations automatically send these data 20 times a second to the test ban treaty organization headquarters in Vienna, where computers pick out potentially interesting events. Scientists need to differentiate between infrasound from a meteor, a volcano, or a nuclear device.

"Ideally, we want to be able to say 'Here we have a signal, and we know it wasn't a nuclear test,'" says Michael A. Hedlin of the Scripps Institution of Oceanography in La Jolla, Calif., who heads the monitoring station in Piñon Flat, Calif.

This wealth of infrasound data isn't bound solely for Vienna. Scientists elsewhere are taking advantage of new infrasound-microphone arrays, both those within the nuclear-test monitoring network and at a handful of independent stations, to listen in on and study a variety of events in the atmosphere.

Last year, for example, 10 monitoring stations in the western United States and Canada recorded the explosion of the space shuttle Columbia. Some observers thought they saw lightning strike the shuttle or meteors explode nearby, but investigators discounted those reports because neither event showed up on infrasonic recordings, says Henry E. Bass of the University of Mississippi. Bass presented the shuttle data at the December 2003 American Geophysical Union meeting in San Francisco.

Hearing Inaudible Noises

Infrasound interpretation is a young science. Acousticians and geophysicists are still learning what phenomena generate infrasound signatures and how to match signatures with phenomena.

For example, John V. Olson of the University of Alaska in Fairbanks recalls one morning last April when a colleague rushed into his office and asked whether he had heard an explosion the night before. The two scientists found a large pulse on the infrasound record from the nuclear-test monitoring station that the university operates and traced it to a nearby firing range. The next day, the local paper reported that a citizen had found a bundle of dynamite, which police exploded at the range.

"So, we take [the signal] out of the 'little green men' file and say, 'This is what dynamite looks like from 5 miles away,'" says Olson. "Slowly, daily, we sift and sort through these signals."

Ocean storms and waves are two of the big generators of infrasound, says Milton A. Garcés of the University of Hawaii, Manoa. The routine up-and-down movements of the waves act as a giant loudspeaker, pushing the air at infrasonic frequencies.

The swirling winds of hurricanes generate different infrasonic signals. Studying the rumblings of gathering storms could eventually lead to better prediction systems, suggests Hedlin. Researchers plan to use a future monitoring station in Cape Verde to study infrasound generated off the coast of western Africa, a known nursery for hurricanes destined for the East Coast of the United States.

Low-frequency sounds are also generated by one of the most colorful displays in the sky, the northern lights, which are caused by charged particles in the air. This electricity heats atmospheric gases, and the warmed gas molecules spread out and increase air pressure.

"It pushes the neutral air forward, almost like the bow wave off a ship," says Olson. This air movement creates an infrasonic signal. The readings are visible during the beginnings of these magnetic storms, as the bright, greenish lights sweep across the sky like a fluttering curtain.

Olson, who presented infrasound data on these auroras at the December American Geophysical Union meeting, says he hopes that scientists can use such findings to better understand the bright lights in the sky.

A less-serene type of atmospheric storm poses a different opportunity for infrasound science. At NASA's Langley Research Center, Zuckerwar is investigating how to use infrasound data to warn airplane pilots of clear-air turbulence. These invisible patches of air are associated with jet streams and cause the bumpy plane rides that pilots try to avoid.

"Today, there's only one way to detect atmospheric turbulence, and that's when a pilot flies into it," Zuckerwar says. Currently, computer models can forecast clear-air turbulence, but there's no direct detection device.

Zuckerwar and his colleagues set up an array of four infrasonic microphones at the NASA facility. Bright orange casings protect the microphones from wind, which is one of the biggest problems for acoustic researchers. Much work went into finding the polyurethane material, which lets in infrasound but blocks the wind.

The microphones constantly record infrasonic wavelengths that pass over the arrays, and once a week the researchers download the collected data. Then, one member of the team looks for patterns in the infrasound record that correspond to pilot reports of turbulence or predicted turbulent areas within a 300-kilometer range of the microphones. The researchers haven't reported any infrasound signatures yet.

Although Zuckerwar emphasizes that the research is in an early phase, his goal is to establish infrasonic monitoring stations, probably one every 200 km or so turbulence-prone areas. Flight controllers would pick out characteristic turbulence readings and quickly notify pilots of the hazard.

Ear to the Ground

While specialized microphones can pick up infrasonic signals generated high in the atmosphere, they detect more earthly rumbles, as well. For instance, Jeffrey B. Johnson of the University of Hawaii at Manoa, has placed microphones within a kilometer of a vent of the active Erebus volcano in Antarctica. The sensors have recorded low-frequency signals so powerful that, were they audible, they'd have a volume in excess of 130 decibels—"somewhere between a jet airplane and the threshold of pain," says Johnson. Erebus does produce some audible sound, but it's not very loud, he says.

The infrasound radiating from the volcano's lava lake is generated by the rupture of 10-meter-wide, gas-filled bubbles, which pushes huge infrasound waves into the atmosphere. Johnson can use infrasound readings to estimate the size of the lava bubbles within Erebus and the amount of gas they contain.

"Infrasound is a powerful tool to understand more about explosions and eruption sources," says Johnson. "It allows us to directly quantify what's going on at a volcanic vent."

Studying the patterns of infrasound that precede eruptions might also have predictive value. While placing infrasound sensors on the Sakurajima volcano in Japan, Garcés witnessed an unexpected series of increasingly frequent and powerful explosions. By the end of the day, Sakurajima erupted.

"We collected some really good data," said Garcés, "and demonstrated there is a relationship between the increasing amplitude of a wave and how often these events occur" leading up to an eruption.

If researchers monitoring a volcano learn when it's about to erupt, they could warn nearby residents and pilots scheduled to fly in the vicinity. The eruption endangers people on the ground and spews volcanic ash that could bring down a jet.

Tests are under way to use infrasound data as a warning signal for avalanches as well. When snow rushes down mountains, it pushes air before it and creates infrasound at frequencies below 8 Hz.

Ernie Scott of IML Air Science in Sheridan, Wyo., set up infrasound-detecting microphones in Teton Pass, Wyo., an area prone to avalanches. State officials there frequently set off explosives to create minor cascades that defuse snow buildup. Scott recorded these triggered avalanches and used the patterns to design a prototype detection system for the Wyoming Department of Transportation. This winter, the agency will use the system to monitor activity over a one-square-mile area of Teton Pass, where avalanches are a frequent wintertime hazard to skiers and drivers. The data will be converted to radio signals transmitted to highway personnel 15 miles away.

"Essentially, they can sit there and listen for an avalanche to occur," says Scott. "If it hits a highway, they can send the road crews out."

An infrasound monitoring system could also immediately alert rescue units of avalanches that may have trapped skiers.

The goal of IML Air Science is to market an avalanche detection device to snowy states and countries.

Whether infrasound is used for commercial purposes, to learn more about natural phenomena, or simply to listen for something that nobody wants to hear, it is entering what those in the field call a renaissance. Geophysicists and acousticians are sorting through, categorizing, and studying a wide range of inaudible noise. Says Bass: "Everybody out here is excited about something different."

Animal Acoustics

Just because people can't hear infrasound doesn't mean other animals can't. In the early 1980s, Katy Payne of Cornell University and her colleagues found that elephants' rumbling vocalizations contain pressure waves at frequencies as low as 14 hertz that can travel up to 10 kilometers across forests and savannas. The researchers suggested that elephants communicate over long distances via infrasound.

It's still unclear how elephants create or detect infrasound, but Caitlin E. O'Connell-Rodwell of Stanford University is examining the idea that an infrasound portion of elephant calls is transmitted through the ground to be picked up by distant elephants' feet.

"We noticed a pattern of behavior before the arrival of an [infrasonic] event," says O'Connell-Rodwell. The elephants "shift the weight on their feet and lean forward, as if they were paying attention to the ground with their feet," she says. O'Connell-Rodwell and her colleagues found that elephant rumblings cause waves that propagate through the ground as well as through the air. The seismic waves, which can travel 4 kilometers to 16 km, may extend the reach of elephant communication.

Low-frequency communications have also been linked to whales and rhinos—other large animals that produce powerful sounds. Some scientists have hypothesized that dinosaurs could generate and pick up infrasound. Now, research suggests that some birds create these ultrabass notes as well.

In the October 2003 *Auk*, Andrew L. Mack of the Wildlife Conservation Society in Papua New Guinea and Josh Jones, now of Scripps Institution of Oceanography in La Jolla, Calif., report that the large, flightless cassowary emits borderline-infrasonic calls as low as 23 Hz.

Cassowaries live solitary lives in the rain forests of Papua New Guinea and Australia, and Mack proposes that their deep sounds reach neighbors and potential mates through thick vegetation. He's currently investigating how cassowaries detect infrasound, paying particular attention to the large, pointy casque atop each bird's head.

While people can't hear infrasound, they apparently detect it in other ways. Mack describes a "strange sort of sensation" from standing near a calling cassowary, and O'Connell-Rodwell says that when elephants rumble, "it's such a powerful, low-frequency sound, you really feel it resonating in your chest."

A recent acoustic experiment in England tested people's responses to unrecognized infrasound. A team of acousticians, psychologists, and musicians rigged a large pipe to produce 17-Hz waves, which they played during selected contemporary music pieces being performed in a concert hall. The 750 concertgoers later answered questions about emotions or strange feelings that they may have experienced during the pieces. The scientists presented their findings in September 2003 at the British Association for the Advancement of Science's Festival of Science at the University of Salford in England.

During pieces accompanied by infrasound, "the effect was to intensify the current emotional state" of the listeners, says acoustician Richard Lord of the National Physical Laboratory in Teddington, England. The investigators suggest this could explain why some pipe organ music can elicit powerful emotions in people.

The manatee is a gentle plant-eating creature that lives in the warm, shallow waters throughout Florida, a habitat it now shares with humans.

Humans, unfortunately, access these waters most often in boats with underwater propellers, a situation that poses an extreme hazard for the manatees. It has long been a puzzle why boats and manatees collide so often, to the detriment of the manatees, even though it might seem that the manatees have the ability to hear and recognize the danger of the approaching boats.

Enter the science of bioacoustics. Edmund R. Gerstein, director of marine mammal research at Florida Atlantic University, describes how he and his wife spent many years asking the questions of how the manatees hear the boats approaching, how they determine the direction of approach, and under what acoustic conditions they can hear the boats. The answers they discovered, through careful acoustic measurements of the manatee habitats, boat noise, and the hearing abilities of manatees, were not in agreement with the standing assumptions that determine boating policies in the area. —LCK

From "Manatees, Bioacoustics and Boats"
by Edmund R. Gerstein
American Scientist, **March/April 2002**

It's 2 o'clock in the morning, and, wouldn't you know it, Stormy is "in love" with that big Navy transducer again. Now I have to get in the cold water and pry him off so we can set up for Dundee's session. Oh, the joys of working with manatees under the Tampa moonlight! Even though I'll be tired, cold and wet, before sunrise we will have measured another critical aspect of the Florida manatee's hearing abilities. Over the next seven years of extended late-night auditory testing—more than 30,000 threshold trials in all—my wife Laura and I will measure two teenage manatees' ability to hear, locate and discriminate different underwater signals under various controlled acoustical conditions. In the end, we will have laid the groundwork for a sensory explanation for why manatees are hit repeatedly by boats.

The endangered Florida manatee, a subspecies of the West Indian manatee *(Trichechus manatus)*, is a gentle, bewhiskered herbivore that can reach 4 meters in length, weigh up to 1,300 kilograms and live over 60 years. Designated as Florida's official marine mammal, the manatee has been the focus of more controversy and polarization over conservation and protection than perhaps any other mammal. "Sea cows," as they are sometimes affectionately called, inhabit shallow coastal, estuarine and riverine habitats throughout peninsular Florida, where they graze on sea grasses and are routinely injured and sometimes killed by collisions with recreational boats, barges and commercial ships. These collisions are so prevalent that the majority of wild manatees are identified by their characteristic boat scars.

After more than two decades of manatee-protection policies that have focused on slowing boats passing through manatee habitats, the number of injuries and deaths associated with collisions has increased and reached record highs in the past two years. To help track the population, Florida and federal wildlife agencies maintain a growing scar catalogue of recognized living individuals who have survived collisions. Some of these manatees have propeller wounds from as many as 16 different boat strikes. Why does this happen?

When startled or frightened, manatees explode with a burst of power and can reach swimming speeds of up to 6.4 meters per second in an instant. My colleagues and I wondered: Given that manatees have the cognitive ability to recognize danger, a fear-flight reaction and the physical prowess to evade boats, why, after an individual has been hit once, twice or three times, doesn't it learn to avoid boats? Is it possible that manatees are unaware of the danger? Can they hear boats approaching, and if so, from how far away, from which direction and under what acoustic conditions?

These basic questions suggested a number of inter-disciplinary behavioral and acoustic investigations that I conducted over the past decade with Joseph E. Blue, retired director of the Naval Undersea Warfare Center and the Naval Research Laboratory's Underwater Sound Reference Detachment and now president of Leviathan Legacy, Inc.; Steven E. Forsythe of the Naval Undersea Warfare Center; and Laura. No one had previously conducted rigorous, controlled underwater psychoacoustic (audiometric) studies, which are nec-essary to understand what sounds manatees can hear in their environment. In conjunction with audiometric studies, we conducted a comprehensive series of under-water acoustic surveys of various wild manatee habitats, along with critical boat-noise propagation measurements, to further understand why animals are so vulnerable to collisions. Defining and applying the physics of near-surface acoustic propagation are also necessary if collisions between boats and animals are to be reduced, not only in Florida's aquatic byways but also on the open seas, where great whales are regularly injured and often killed by large ships.

Our test results contradict several long-held beliefs that form the basis of current protection strategies. Manatees have good hearing abilities at high frequencies, however, they have relatively poor sensitivity in the low frequency ranges associated with boat noise. Ironically, manatees may be *least* able to hear the propellers of boats that have slowed down in compliance with boat speed regulations intended to reduce collisions. Such noise often fails to rise above the noisy background in manatee habitats until the boat is literally on top of the manatee. In addition, near-surface boundary effects can cancel or severely attenuate the dominant low-frequency sound produced by propellers. In many situations, ship noise is not projected in directional paths where hearing these sounds could help the animals avoid collisions. Our basic and applied research results suggest that there may be a technological solution to address the underlying root causes of the collision problem and resolve the clash between human and animal interests.

The Manatee Hearing Test

In 1991 we initiated experiments with two captive-born manatees, Stormy and Dundee, at the Lowry Park Zoo in Tampa. Our first objective was to define an *audiogram*—that is, to map the absolute hearing abilities of these subjects under very quiet conditions. The audiogram or hearing curve is a graph that demonstrates the overall range of frequencies an individual can hear as well as the subject's sensitivity within this range. An audiogram plots the intensity of a signal at its minimal detection threshold. The resultant plot for most mammals is U-shaped, with the lowest thresholds depicting the greatest sensitivity. The highest thresholds (areas of least sensitivity) are found at the low and high ends of the frequency range, where greater intensity or volume is necessary to reach detection thresholds.

Before we began testing manatees' hearing and making acoustic measurements of their habitats and boat noise, most of the wildlife biologists and managers charged with protecting manatees assumed the animals could readily hear boats but were just too slow or not smart enough to learn to avoid watercraft. Earlier electro-physiological measurements conducted by Ted Bullock, Tom O'Shea and John McClune in 1982 and anatomical measurements of dead manatees reported in 1992 by Darlene Ketten, Dan Odell and Darryl Domning had suggested that manatees heard *best* at low frequencies, in the 1,000- to 5,000-hertz range, and therefore could readily detect the sounds of boats. However, since hearing is a perceptual phenomenon, the most accurate way to find out what an animal can truly hear is to ask it. Hence the behavioral audiogram is recognized as the definitive measurement of hearing . . .

Being the first to train manatees for psychoacoustic testing, we didn't know their overall visual acuity, nor did we know which modality or weighted combination of modalities manatees might rely on the most. Therefore, I constructed the hearing test using a forced two-choice paradigm with two response paddles that were distinctly different both visually and tactually—one paddle was smooth, with a striped black-and-white pattern, the other solid white with a rough surface and a distinctly different-shaped end made of intersecting pipe sections. Both manatees were trained to position themselves inside a listening station (a hoop) where an underwater microphone, or hydrophone, recorded the signals sent to them. They were to stay in the hoop, listen and wait for a strobe light to flash. After the light flashed they could leave the hoop and select the striped paddle if they heard a sound ("yes"), or the solid white one if they did not detect a sound ("no"). These tests were repeated for many different types of sounds, including boat noise against various sound levels typical of wild ambient conditions.

We used a conventional staircase method of double-blind signal presentations, starting with very loud acoustic levels (at which the manatee would choose the "tone" paddle), stepping down the signal amplitude until the animal chose the "no tone" paddle and then stepping it back up again. Hundreds of trials were required to establish the threshold for each frequency point along the curve. The resulting audiograms for the two manatees were very similar . . .

As the audiogram illustrates [see Figure 3 on page 92], manatees have a functional hearing range from 400 to 46,000 hertz. Their peak sensitivity actually lies between 16,000 and 18,000 hertz, and not 1,000 to 5,000 hertz as previously thought. Below 16,000 hertz sensitivity

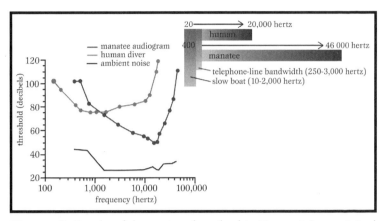

Figure 3. Results of the testing described in Figure 2 [see original article for illustration] were consistent from one manatee to the other and produced the audiogram curve presented on a logarithmic scale [above]. The manatees' hearing thresholds at each frequency are measured in decibels against a reference sound pressure of 1 micropascal, the underwater standard. The animals' best sensitivity in the quiet ambient conditions of the test pool was at 16,000 to 18,000 hertz. Below 1,000 hertz they required much louder sounds to hear. Many people assumed that since people can hear boats underwater, surely manatees could as well. However, people hear low-frequency sounds much better than manatees, both underwater and in air (linear scale, above).

decreases approximately 10 decibels per octave, and below 2,000 hertz it drops precipitously (20 decibels per octave) until functional hearing ends at 400 hertz. Unfortunately the dominant sounds produced by most boats and ships are below 1,000 hertz; these lower frequencies fall outside or overlap the lower fringe of the manatees' hearing range. The audiogram suggests that even in quiet conditions, manatees would have difficulty detecting these sounds at acoustic levels less than 90 or 100 decibels . . .

In Search of Solutions

Just as speed limits for small boats in inland waters can reduce propeller noise and sound frequency, so reducing ship speeds could conceivably increase the risk of collision by increasing exposure time (and thus opportunities for collisions) while diminishing the ships' audibility. Current surveillance and avoidance programs are ineffective at night or in poor weather, just when the animals also must rely on sound detection to avoid ships. Today wildlife managers are focused on other protection methods that still do not address the underlying sensory and acoustic causes of collisions. These methods include active sonar to detect animals ahead of ships and passive-listening sensors that light up to indicate that manatees are in the area . . .

We decided that the best way to protect animals would be to address the underlying sensory and acoustical causes of collisions. Manatees and whales may be well adapted to hear and detect significant biological sounds in their environments; however, boats, ships and barges were never part of their evolutionary histories. Thus these animals are faced with modern ecological challenges for which they are at a sensory disadvantage. In light of the psychoacoustic measurements described above, the known acoustical characteristics of shallow-water habitats, the spectra of boat noise and the dangerous, deceptive problem of acoustical shadowing, it is apparent that manatees, and perhaps other passive-listening marine mammals, could benefit from an acoustic warning device designed to fit on the front of boats, ships and barges . . .

For all our custodial efforts and regulations to protect manatees, even the most conscientious and best-intentioned boaters can still strike manatees they cannot see. When an animal cannot hear or locate a boat, it is at risk whether the boat is going fast or slow. In the end, the most reliable, motivated and responsive individual that can save any manatee at any place and time is the manatee itself—provided it has the sensory awareness to do so. An acoustic alerting device could give animals the opportunity to save themselves.

Reprinted with permission from *American Scientist*.

Electromagnetic Waves Interacting with Matter

5

Electronic tools, such as computers, media, and communication devices, based on semiconductor physics are ubiquitous, found in every home, car, industry, and classroom. The physics behind this explosion of applied science is rooted in the way in which electrons flow through semiconductor crystals. On a small scale, the relative geometric order of the semiconductor atoms dictates what kinds of energies the electrons may have and what energies they cannot have. This property, the band gap structure of semiconductors, has been exploited by scientists and engineers to create the modern technological society. Now, physicists Greg G. Parker and Martin Charlton explain how similar properties of light traveling through artificially constructed and ordered materials called photonic crystals promises to create a similar boom in technology, this time based on the passage of light and not electrons. The excitement of this promise lies in the fact that we have greater control over the properties

of the artificially created photonic crystals than we ever had over the electronic properties of semiconductors. —LCK

From "Photonic Crystals"
by Greg G. Parker and M. Charlton
Physics World, August 2000

Since the 1970s the number of electronic components that can be fitted onto a microchip has doubled every 18 months, allowing computers to double in speed, or half in price, during the same period. Although this trend—which was predicted by Gordon Moore of Intel in the 1960s—may continue for the next few years, the top speed at which integrated circuits can operate is beginning to level out.

We can now buy personal computers that operate at 1 GHz (10^9 Hz), which is very impressive, but what is the likelihood of a 100 GHz desktop computer appearing on the market? Indeed, given our current understanding of semiconductor technology, even producing a 10 GHz personal computer would seem to be difficult. However, by transmitting signals with light rather than electrons, it might be possible to build a computer that operates at hundreds of terahertz (10^{12} Hz). Researchers now believe that such an awesome processing engine could be built from optical components made from so-called photonic crystals and quasicrystals. These materials have highly periodic structures that can be designed to control and manipulate the propagation of light.

Basics of Photonic Band Gaps

The easiest way to understand the behaviour of light in a photonic crystal is to compare it to the movement of electrons and holes in a semiconductor. In a silicon crystal, for example, the atoms are arranged in a diamond-lattice structure, and electrons moving through this lattice experience a periodic potential as they interact with the silicon nuclei via the Coulomb force. This interaction results in the formation of allowed and forbidden energy states. For pure and perfect silicon crystals, no electrons will be found in an energy range called the forbidden energy gap or simply the band gap. However, the situation is different for real materials: electrons can have an energy within the band gap if the periodicity of the lattice is broken by a missing silicon atom or by an impurity atom occupying a silicon site, or if the material contains interstitial impurities (additional atoms located at non-lattice sites).

Now consider photons moving through a block of transparent dielectric material that contains a number of tiny air holes arranged in a lattice pattern. The photons will pass through regions of high refractive index—the dielectric—interspersed with regions of low refractive index—the air holes. To a photon, this contrast in refractive index looks just like the periodic potential that an electron experiences travelling through a silicon crystal. Indeed, if there is large contrast in refractive index between the two regions then most of the light will be confined either within the dielectric material or the air holes. This confinement results in the formation of allowed energy regions separated by a forbidden region—the so-called photonic band gap. Since the wavelength of the photons is inversely proportional to their energy, the patterned dielectric material will block light with wavelengths in the photonic band gap, while allowing other wavelengths to pass freely.

It is possible to create energy levels in the photonic band gap by changing the size of a few of the air holes in the material. This is the photonic equivalent to breaking the perfect periodicity of the silicon-crystal lattice. In this case, the diameter of the air holes is a critical parameter, together with the contrast in refractive index throughout the material.

Photonic band gap structures can also be made from a lattice of high-refractive-index material embedded within a medium with a lower refractive index. A naturally occurring example of such a material is opal. However, the contrast in the refractive index in opal is rather small, which results in a rather small band gap.

The potential of photonic-crystal structures was first realized in 1987 by Eli Yablonovitch, then at Bell Communications Research in New Jersey. A few years later in 1991, Yablonovitch and co-workers produced the first photonic crystal by mechanically drilling holes a millimetre in diameter into a block of material with a refractive index of 3.6. The material, which became known as "Yablonovite," prevented microwaves from propagating in any direction—in other words, it exhibited a 3-D photonic band gap. Other structures that have band gaps at microwave and radio frequencies are currently being used to make antennae that direct radiation away from the heads of mobile-phone users.

In spite of this success, it has taken over a decade to fabricate photonic crystals that work in the near-infrared (780–3000 nm) and visible (450–750 nm) regions of the spectrum. The main challenge has been to find suitable materials and processing techniques to fabricate structures that are about a thousandth the size of microwave crystals.

A rough estimate of the spacing between the air holes (or the lattice size) is given by the wavelength of the light divided by the refractive index of the dielectric material. The problem in making small structures is compounded because it is more favourable for a photonic band gap to form in dielectrics with a high refractive index, which reduces the size of the lattice spacing even further. For example, suppose we wanted to create a photonic crystal that could trap near-infrared light with a wavelength of 1 µm in a material with a refractive index of 3.0. We would have to create a structure in which the air holes were separated by about 0.3 µm—an extremely difficult task. If the scale was 1,000 times smaller, we could build the structure atom-by-atom using a chemical reaction; and if it was 1,000 times larger we could build the structure mechanically, as Yablonovitch and co-workers did.

To be able to create photonic crystals for optical devices, we need to use state-of-the-art semiconductor-microfabrication techniques with their associated high production costs and investment. For this reason computer modelling of prospective photonic-crystal structures is also a very important area of research, as it may prevent expensive fabrication errors later.

Optical Communications

So why are photonic crystals generating so much interest? Again it is useful to draw analogies with silicon. The current explosion in information technology has been derived from our ability to control the flow of electrons in a semiconductor in the most intricate ways. Photonic crystals promise to give us similar control over photons—with even greater flexibility because we have far more control over the properties of photonic crystals than we do over the electronic properties of semiconductors. Given the impact that semiconductor materials have had on every sector of society, photonic crystals could play an even greater role in the 21st century, particularly in the optical-communications industry.

In current communications systems, audio or video signals are encoded as streams of digital data packets. These voltage pulses are applied to a light-emitting diode (LED) or a semiconductor laser, which converts them into short pulses of light that are then sent along an optical-fibre network. Many different conversations or video signals can be transmitted using a single wavelength of light by interweaving the data packets from different sources, a technique known as time-division multiplexing. The optical data pulses are sorted at the receiving end of the fibre, where they are converted by photodetectors into continuous analogue electrical signals that are then transmitted along copper wires.

A simple way of increasing the amount of data that can be transmitted by a single optical fibre is to make the incoming electronic pulses as short as possible. Current optical systems have achieved data rates in excess of 40 gigabits per second. But to increase this value significantly will require cheap, bright LEDs that can be switched on and off at very high speed.

Another way to increase the capacity of the fibre is to add new signals at other optical wavelengths, a method known as dense wavelength division multiplexing (DWDM). However, the optical fibre is only transparent over a small range of wavelengths, so the number of separate conversations that can be transmitted depends on the linewidth of neighbouring optical channels (which is currently at the sub-nanometre level). Encoding and sorting thousands of such channels poses quite a problem: at the transmitting end of the system, each wavelength channel requires a very stable light source that only emits in a very narrow range of wavelengths. Although LEDs offer high switching speeds, they emit light over a wide range of wavelengths, which makes them less suitable than lasers for DWDM systems.

At the receiving end, very narrow linewidth filters and optical switches are required to separate individual channels and then route them to the appropriate destinations. Due to the large number of individual components in a DWDM system, it makes sense to combine as many of them as possible onto an "integrated" optical chip. This would reduce both the amount of costly manual work that is needed to build the system and the number of possible points where it could fail.

Such integration, however, raises other problems. First we need to develop small-scale optical "interconnects"— tiny planar waveguides that can steer light round tight corners. While it is straightforward to route electrons round sharp bends in microchips, it is impossible to direct light in the same way using conventional glass waveguides because the losses at the bends are so large.

Photonic crystals could address many of the problems that currently limit the speed and capacity of optical-communications networks. For example, these structures could be used to create novel LEDs and lasers that emit light in a very narrow wavelength range, together with highly selective optical filters that could be integrated on a chip.

Photonic Crystals Light the Way

Light-emitting diodes play a key role in optical-communication systems. These devices are made from so-called photoemissive materials that emit photons once they have been excited electrically or optically. These photons are typically emitted in many different directions and also have a range of wavelengths, which is not ideal for communications applications. We can create an LED that only emits light in the forward direction by placing a reflector behind the photoemissive layer. However, the efficiency of such a device is limited by the efficiency of the reflector.

Photonic crystals could be used to design a mirror that reflects a selected wavelength of light from any angle with high efficiency. Moreover, they could be integrated within the photoemissive layer to create an LED that emits light at a specific wavelength and direction.

Ideally we need to build a truly 3-D lattice structure to gain complete control of the light in all three dimensions. Several ingenious ways to produce these so-called 3-D photonic crystals have recently been devised in addition to Yablonovitch's method. For example, in 1994 Ekmel Özbay, then at the Ames Laboratory in the US, and co-workers fabricated a photonic crystal with a band gap at microwave wavelengths by stacking micromachined silicon wafers in a "woodpile" or "picket fence" structure [figure 1].

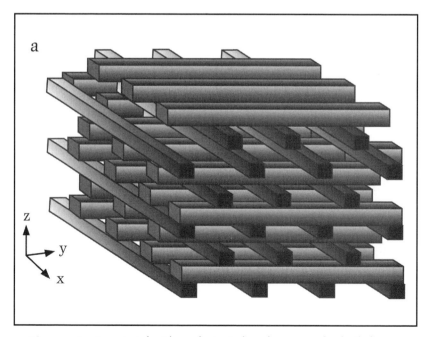

Figure 1. A material with a photonic band gap can be built from a lattice made of layers of micromachined silicon "matchsticks."

The key to their success was the accurate alignment of successive layers—inaccurate alignment destroys the band gap. However, it becomes increasingly difficult to achieve the required accuracy as the dimensions of the structure are reduced, and as the number of layers is increased, in an attempt to make a device that operates at optical wavelengths . . .

Fortunately 2-D periodic lattices exhibit some of the useful properties of a truly 3-D photonic crystal, and are far simpler to make. These structures can block certain wavelengths of light at any angle in the plane of the device, and can even prevent light entering from certain angles in the third dimension (i.e. perpendicular to the surface). Thus 2-D photonic crystals are a good compromise for many applications and are easily incorporated within planar waveguides . . .

Future Outlook

Predictions are always difficult to make—however, the future for photonic-crystal circuits and devices looks certain. Within five years a number of basic applications will start making an appearance in the market-place. Among these will be highly efficient photonic-crystal lasers and extremely bright LEDs. On the same timescale we hope to have demonstrated the feasibility of using photonic-crystal waveguides to route light round micron-sized optical benches, and the use of photonic crystals for high-resolution spectral filtering. These demonstrators may be combined to produce a commercially viable "spectrometer on a chip" within a ten-year timescale. Meanwhile, circuits of a similar complexity—including "add-drop filters" and Mach-Zehnder interferometers, common components in optics—will be available at about the same time.

By the time every home is connected to an optical-fibre network, "set-top boxes" that sort and decode the signals will contain photonic-crystal circuits and devices rather than cumbersome optical fibres and silicon circuits. And on a five- to ten-year timescale we should have demonstrated the first photonic-crystal "diodes" and "transistors." A demonstration of the first photonic-crystal logic circuit could even take place in the next 10 to 15 years, while a prototype optical computer driven by photonic crystals could be available within the next 25 years. Surprisingly, synthetic opals could even find a niche in the valuable jewellery and artwork markets, while thin photonic-crystal films could also be used as anti-counterfeit devices on credit cards.

If our predictions are hopelessly awry, by then we hope that most people will have forgotten we made them. Nevertheless the future for photonic crystals looks bright.

Reprinted with permission from *Physics World*.

When a wave passes from one substance to another, such as when light passes from water to air, the speed of the wave changes. This change in wave speed causes the wave to travel at different angles in the two media. This deflection is known as refraction, and it is familiar to most people when looking into a pool of water. It is the refraction of light that makes a reed of grass appear to bend as it passes from the water into the air, and it is the relative refractive index n between the two media that determines the degree of bending. Light is an electromagnetic wave, and so the refractive index is closely related to the ability of the material to respond to electrical charges (the permittivity ε) and magnetic fields (permeability μ). This article makes a few challenging mathematical relations between ε and μ to show that it is possible for the refractive index of a material to be negative, which leads to interesting consequences.

John Pendry, a professor of physics at Imperial College in London, England, and David Smith, an adjunct professor of physics at the University of California, San Diego, tell how fabricated "metamaterials" can have a negative refractive index. These human-made materials exhibit the reversal of wave refraction, and the authors explain how this property can be used in compact negative-index lenses, for example. —LCK

From "Reversing Light with Negative Refraction"
by John B. Pendry and David R. Smith
Physics Today, June 2004

Victor Veselago, in a paper[1] published in 1968, pondered the consequences for electromagnetic waves interacting with a hypothetical material for which both the electric permittivity ε and the magnetic permeability μ were simultaneously negative. Because no naturally occurring material or compound has ever been demonstrated with negative ε and μ, Veselago wondered whether this apparent asymmetry in material properties was just happenstance or perhaps had a more fundamental origin. He concluded that not only should such materials be possible, but if ever found, they would exhibit remarkable properties unlike those of any known materials and would give a twist to virtually all electromagnetic phenomena. Foremost among these properties is a negative index of refraction . . .

Although somewhat less common than positive materials, negative materials are nevertheless easy to find. Materials with negative ε include metals (such as silver, gold, and aluminum) at optical frequencies; materials with negative μ include resonant ferromagnetic or antiferromagnetic systems . . .

Metamaterials Extend Material Response

Because of the seeming separation in frequency between electric and magnetic resonant phenomena, Veselago's analysis of materials with ε and μ both negative might have remained a curious exercise in electromagnetic theory. However, in the mid-1990s, researchers began looking into the possibility of engineering artificial materials to have a tailored electromagnetic response. Although the field of artificial materials dates back to the 1940s, advances in fabrication and computation—coupled with the emerging awareness of the importance of negative materials—led to a resurgence of effort in developing new structures with novel material properties.

To form an artificial material, we start with a collection of repeated elements designed to have a strong response to applied electromagnetic fields. As long as the size and spacing of the elements are much smaller than the electromagnetic wavelengths of interest, incident radiation cannot distinguish the collection of elements from a homogeneous material. We can thus conceptually replace the inhomogeneous composite by a continuous material described by material parameters ε and μ. At lower frequencies, conductors are excellent candidates from which to form artificial materials, because their response to electromagnetic fields is large . . .

Negative Refraction

Maxwell's equations determine how electromagnetic waves propagate within a medium and can be solved to arrive at a wave equation of the form

$$\frac{\partial^2 E(x,t)}{\partial x^2} = \varepsilon\mu \, \frac{\partial^2 E(x,t)}{\partial t^2}.$$

In this equation, ε and μ enter as a product, so it would not appear to matter whether their signs were both positive or both negative. Indeed, solutions of the wave equation have the form $\exp[i(nkd - \omega t)]$, where $n = \sqrt{\varepsilon\mu}$ is the refractive index. Propagating solutions exist in the material whether ε and μ are both positive or both negative. So what, if anything, is the difference between positive and negative materials?

It turns out that one needs to be more careful in taking the square root, because ε and μ are analytic functions whose values are generally complex. There is an ambiguity in the sign of the square root that is resolved by a proper analysis. For example, if instead of writing $\varepsilon = -1$ and $\mu = -1$ we write $\varepsilon = \exp(i\pi)$ and $\mu = \exp(i\pi)$, then $n = \sqrt{\varepsilon\mu} = \exp(i\pi/2)\exp(i\pi/2) = \exp(i\pi) = -1$. The important step is that the square root of either ε or μ alone must have a positive imaginary part—a necessity for a passive material.

This briefly stated argument shows why the material Veselago pondered years ago is so unique: The index of refraction is negative. A negative refractive index implies that the phase of a wave decreases rather than advances with passage through the medium. As Veselago pointed out, this fundamental reversal of wave propagation contains important implications for nearly all electromagnetic phenomena. Many of the exotic effects of negative index have been or are currently being pursued by researchers. But perhaps the most immediately accessible phenomenon from an experimental or computational point of view is the reversal of wave refraction, illustrated in figure 2.

Figure 2

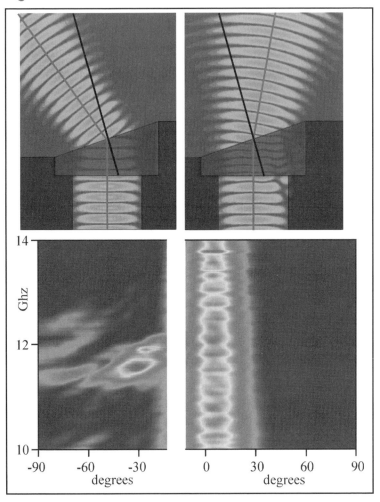

Snell's law, which describes quantitatively the bending of a wave as it enters a medium, is perhaps one of the oldest and most well known of electromagnetic phenomena. In the form of a wedge refraction experiment, as depicted in figure 2, Snell's law is also the basis for a direct measurement of a material's refractive index.

Figure 2. A negative-index material will refract light through a negative angle. **(a)** In this simulation[17] of a Snell's law experiment, a negative-index wedge with $\varepsilon = -1$ and $\mu = -1$ deflects an electromagnetic beam by a negative angle relative to the surface normal: The beam emerges on the same side of the surface normal as the incident beam. Color [see original article] represents intensity: [gray line], highest; [black line], lowest. **(b)** A positive-index wedge, in contrast, will positively refract the same beam. [Gray] lines trace the path of the beams, and the surface normals are shown in black. Experiments confirm this behavior. **(c)** The deflection angle (horizontal axis) observed for a beam traversing a negative wedge as a function of frequency (vertical axis). **(d)** The deflection angle observed for a positive-index Teflon® wedge as a function of frequency. In the negative wedge there is strong dispersion with frequency: The condition $\varepsilon = -1$, $\mu = -1$ is realized only over a narrow bandwidth around 12 GHz.

In this type of experiment, a wave is incident normal to a wedge-shaped sample. The wave is transmitted through the transparent sample and strikes the second interface at an angle. Because of the difference in refractive index between the material and free space, the beam exits the wedge deflected by some angle from the direction of incidence.

One might imagine that an experimental determination of Snell's law would be a simple matter. The peculiarities of metamaterials, however, add a layer of complexity that renders the experimental confirmation somewhat more difficult. Present samples, based on SRRs and wires, are frequency dispersive with fairly narrow bandwidths and exhibit considerable loss. The first experiment showing negative refraction was performed in 2001 by one of us (Smith) and colleagues at the University of California, San Diego.[3] In an experiment similar to that depicted in figure 2, they measured the power refracted from a two-dimensional wedge-shaped metamaterial sample as a function of angle, confirming the expected properties . . .

Although it has proven to be a valuable concept, a rigorously defined negative index of refraction may not necessarily be a prerequisite for negative-refraction phenomena. An alternate approach to attaining negative refraction uses the properties of photonic crystals,[6, 7] materials that lie on the transition between a metamaterial and an ordinary structured dielectric. Photonic crystals derive their properties from Bragg reflection in a periodic structure engineered in the body of a dielectric, typically by drilling or etching holes. The periodicity in photonic crystals is on the order of the wavelength, so that the distinction between refraction and diffraction is blurred. Nevertheless, with photonic crystals many novel dispersion relationships can be realized, including ranges in which the frequency disperses negatively with wave vector as required for a negative refraction. Using photonic crystals,[8, 9] researchers have observed focusing, as predicted for negative-index materials . . .

A Better Focus

Refraction is the phenomenon responsible for lenses and similar devices that focus or shape radiation. Although usually thought of in the context of visible light, lenses are utilized throughout the electromagnetic spectrum; they thus represent a good starting point to implement negative index materials.

In his early paper, Veselago noted that a negative-index focusing lens would need to be concave rather than convex—a seemingly trivial matter, but there is more to the story. For thin lenses, geometrical optics—valid for either positive or negative index—gives the result that the focal length f is related to the lens's radius of curvature, R, by $f = R/(n - 1)$. The denominator in the focal-length formula implies an inherent distinction between positive- and negative-index lenses: A material with $n = +1$ does not refract electromagnetic fields, whereas a material with $n = -1$ does. The result is that negative-index lenses can be more compact, with a host of other benefits . . .

Making a conventional lens with the best possible resolution requires a wide aperture. Each ray emanating from an object, as shown in figure 4a, has wave vector components along the axis of the lens, $k_z = k_0\cos\theta$, and perpendicular to the axis, $k_x = k_0\sin\theta$, where k_0 is the wavenumber and θ is the angle of the ray with respect to the axis. The axial projection k_z is responsible for transporting the light from object to image; k_x represents a Fourier component of the image. For good resolution, the larger one can make k_x, the better. The best that can be achieved is $k_x = k_0$, and hence the resolution limit is $\Delta \approx \pi/k_0 = \Lambda/2$, where Λ is the wavelength. This restriction is a huge problem in many areas of optics. The feature size achieved in computer chips and the storage capacity of DVDs, for example, are wavelength-limited. Even a modest relaxation of the wavelength limitation would be of great value.

113

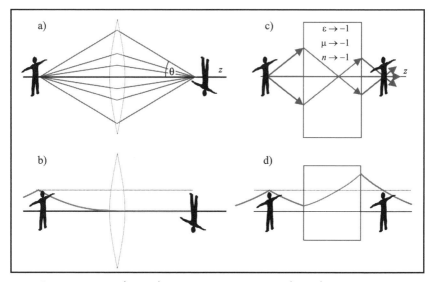

Figure 4. Resolution limitations. **(a)** For good resolution, conventional lenses need a wide aperture to refract rays at large angles θ, but even so, they are limited in resolution by the wavelength used. **(b)** The missing Fourier components of the image are contained in the near field, which decays exponentially [dark gray curve] and makes negligible contribution to the image. **(c)** A lens made from a planar slab of negative-index material not only brings rays to a focus but has the capacity **(d)** to amplify the near field so that it contributes to the image. Such a negative lens thus removes the wavelength limitation. However, the resonant nature of the amplification places severe demands on materials: They must be very low loss.

In contrast to the image, the object has no limit to its electromagnetic details, but unfortunately not all of that information makes it across the lens to the image. The problem lies with the wave vector's z-component, which we can write as $k_z = \sqrt{k_0^2 - k_x^2}$. Evidently, for large values of k_x, corresponding to fine details in the object, k_z is imaginary and the waves decay exponentially as $\exp(-\sqrt{k_x^2 - k_0^2}z)$, as shown in figure 4b. By the time these so-called evanescent waves reach the image, they have negligible amplitude. For that reason, they are commonly referred to as the "near field" and the propagating rays as the "far field."

If by some magic we could amplify the near fields, we could in principle recoup their contribution, but the amplification would have to be of just the right amount and possibly very strong for the most localized components. That is a tall order, but by a remarkable chance, a planar slab of negative material achieves this feat.[12]

Figure 4c shows rays contributing to the image formed by a negative slab. Just as for a conventional lens, the rays only contribute details greater than about half a wavelength in diameter. In contrast, the behavior of the near field is remarkably different, as shown in figure 4d. The near field has the capacity to excite short-wavelength resonances of the negative-index surface that are akin to the surface plasmons on the surfaces of metals such as silver. Interaction with the plasmonlike excitation kicks the decaying wave into a growing wave. The negative medium thus amplifies the wave and compensates for the decay that occurred in an equal thickness of vacuum. The resonances have a finite width and the requirement of $\varepsilon = -1$ and $\mu = -1$ can be met only at one frequency because of the inherent dispersion of negative media. Therefore, this super lensing effect is a narrow-band phenomenon . . .

Building on the Foundations

Negative refraction is a subject with constant capacity for surprise: Innocent assumptions lead to unexpected and sometimes profound consequences. This new field has generated great enthusiasm but also controversy, yet even the controversies have had the positive effect that key concepts have been critically scrutinized in the past 18 months. In the past year, experimental data have been produced that validate the concepts. As a result, we have a firm foundation on which to build.[15] Many groups are already moving forward with applications. The microwave area has naturally been most productive, because the metamaterials required are easier to fabricate. In addition to microwave lenses, novel waveguides and other devices are under consideration.

One of the most exciting possibilities is imaging beyond the wavelength limit. Practical applications will require low-loss materials, which are a great challenge to the designers of new metamaterials. Proposals to employ thin silver films as lenses are being explored in several laboratories. And the challenges are not purely experimental: We are not yet done with theory, because the assumption of negative refraction has many ramifications that are still being explored and are sure to cast more light on this strange but fascinating subject. Not surprisingly, many researchers are joining the field: 2003 saw more than 200 papers published on negative refraction. We expect even more in 2004!

References

1. V. G. Veselago, *Sov. Phys. Usp.* 10, 509 (1968).
2. J. B. Pendry, A. J. Holden, D. J. Robbins, W. J. Stewart, *IEEE Trans. Microwave Theory Tech.* 47, 2075 (1999).
3. R. A. Shelby, D. R. Smith, S. Schultz, *Science* 292, 77 (2001).
4. A. A. Houck, J. B. Brock, I. L. Chuang, *Phys. Rev. Lett.* 90, 137401 (2003).
5. C. G. Parazzoli, R. B. Greegor, K. Li, B. E. C. Koltenbah, M. Tanielian, *Phys. Rev. Lett.* 90, 107401 (2003).

6. M. Notomi, *Phys. Rev. B* 62, 10696 (2000).

7. C. Luo, S. G. Johnson, J. D. Joannopoulos, J. B. Pendry, *Opt. Express* 11, 746 (2003).

8. P. V. Parimi, W. T. Lu, P. Vodo, S. Sridhar, *Nature* 426, 404 (2003).

9. E. Cubukcu, K. Aydin, E. Ozbay, S. Foteinopolou, C. M. Soukoulis, *Phys. Rev. Lett.* 91, 207401 (2003).

10. A. Grbic, G. V. Eleftheriades, *Phys. Rev. Lett.* 92, 117403 (2004).

11. L. Liu, C. Caloz, T. Itoh, *Electron. Lett.* 38, 1414 (2002).

12. J. B. Pendry, *Phys. Rev. Lett.* 85, 3966 (2000).

13. N. Fang, Z. Liu, T. J. Yen, X. Zhang, *Opt. Express* 11, 682 (2003).

14. J. B. Pendry, S. A. Ramakrishna, *J. Phys.: Condens. Matter* 14, 6345 (2003).

15. Further reading can be found in a special edition of *Opt. Express*, "Focus Issue: Negative Refraction and Metamaterials," 11, 639–755 (April 2003), and in M. W. McCall, A. Lakhtakia, W. S. Weiglhofer, *Eur. J. Phys.* 23, 353 (2002).

16. R. A. Shelby, D. R. Smith, S. C. Nemat-Nasser, S. Schultz, *Appl. Phys. Lett.* 78, 4 (2001).

17. P. Kolinko, D. R. Smith, *Opt. Express* 11, 640 (2003).

18. C. G. Parazzoli, R. B. Greegor, J. A. Nielson, M. A. Thompson, K. Li, A. M. Vetter, M. H. Tanielian, *Appl. Phys. Lett.* 34, 3232 (2004).

Reprinted with permission from "Reversing Light with Negative Refraction," by Pendry, John B., and David R. Smith, *Physics Today*, June 2004, Vol. 57, No. 6, p. 37. © 2004, American Institute of Physics.

Spectroscopy, the science of studying the light emissions from materials, is widely used in many different fields of science. In this article, science writer Jennifer Ouellette brings us up to date on new developments in spectroscopy, brought about by the availability of ultrafast lasers and pulse shaping techniques. When a flash of light from a femtosecond laser, for example, is used to illuminate a sample, high-speed processes can be detected and the material properties discerned to a higher precision than is possible with ordinary methods. The applications

for such a technique are wide, including tests and measurement in the semiconductor industry, materials characterization, biological analysis, and archaeological dating. —LCK

From "Time-Resolved Spectroscopy Comes of Age"
by Jennifer Ouellette
The Industrial Physicist, **February/March 2004**

Cutting-edge instrumentation is a critical enabler of breakthroughs in every scientific field, and spectroscopy is one of the oldest and most venerated. Time-resolved spectroscopy (TRS) offers a new twist to standard spectroscopic techniques. Although TRS is not new, the development of ultrafast lasers and pulse-shaping techniques, among other innovations, has opened up a wide range of nascent application areas, including test and measurement in the semiconductor industry, materials characterization, biological analysis, and archeological dating.

What exactly constitutes a TRS technique remains somewhat nebulous. Andrew Monkman, a physicist and co-coordinator of the Center for Time-Resolved Spectroscopy (CTRS) at the University of Durham in England, broadly defines a TRS technique as "anything that allows you to measure the temporal dynamics and the kinetics of photophysical processes." As an example, he cites the measurement of how an absorption band or fluorescence emission of a given material decays over time. Essentially, TRS uses something akin to a flash of strobe light to freeze a moment in time and a camera or a pulsed beam of light as a detector. The basic technique differs little from other spectroscopic methods. A sample is excited, most commonly by a pulsed laser, although researchers use other excitation methods as well. The resulting emissions and their decay times are then measured as a function of time, either by an ultrafast detector or a second pulse of laser light—an all-optical method also known as pump-probe spectroscopy. "Most spectroscopic techniques will have some sort of time-resolved aspect, because it is just a question of collecting a sequence of spectroscopic information" says Richard Jackson, senior applications scientist and manager of Fourier transform infrared (FTIR) applications for Bruker Optics (Billerica, MA).

TRS has its roots in the demonstration by cine photography that all four legs of a horse leave the ground when it gallops, a finding made late in the 19th century by photographer Eadweard Muybridge. Although not technically a time-resolved measurement by today's definition, the experiment nonetheless was the precursor to the development of the flash lamp, which made truly time-resolved studies at the microsecond scale possible. The invention of the pulsed ruby laser advanced the technique into the picosecond regime, and today, the use of ultrafast lasers enables scientists to perform experiments in the nanosecond and femtosecond regimes—both time scales of fundamental importance to problems in physics, chemistry, and biology. In fact, the ready availability of affordable pulsed lasers is one reason TRS has grown in popularity among scientists.

"You do not have to spend all your time building lasers to be able to do this technique anymore," says Monkman. "Lasers have just become a tool for doing the spectroscopy."

The advantage of TRS over traditional spectroscopy is that it enables scientists to make more exact measurements of a sample's properties. "Not only do you get the lifetime of the excited state, but you can also separate out two different decaying species because they decay with different lifetimes," explains Monkman. "So even if their emissions strongly overlap, you can use the difference in decay times to separate them."

Applications

TRS has established a solid foothold in chemistry, the discipline that uses it the most. However, other applications are emerging. "There is more and more interest in dynamic processes in general, that is, watching things happen on very short time scales," says Michael Mellon, chief executive officer and general manager of Quantar Technology, Inc. (Santa Cruz, CA), a major supplier of TRS detector systems. "For example, there is a lot of interest in TRS and time-resolved imaging among biologists because the pathways for biological processes are so important to understand, and these are often revealed by looking at photons or other emissions as a function of time." Biologist Friedrich Siebert, for example, heads an interdisciplinary research group at the University of Freiburg in Germany that uses TRS and related techniques to examine the structure and function of proteins—most notably membrane proteins, which make up about 30 % of all proteins in a cell . . .

Monkman's group uses TRS to study materials such as luminescent polymers used to manufacture plastic light-emitting diodes. "It is a very powerful tool to understand how materials work and how they process energy," he says. "It gives us much more information than simply measuring the spectrum of the emission, or the absorption of a particular polymer that we are studying. Because at the end of the day, to build an ideal display, for every electron you put in, you want to get a photon out." Although many scientists jump straight to femtosecond regimes with TRS, Monkman focuses his work on the slower nanosecond time scale in his experiments. "It is kind of the regime that time forgot," he jokes. "We have filled that gap, because to truly understand something, you have to measure it in all time regimes, from the femtosecond to the steady state. Otherwise, you miss too much."

At Montana State University, Lee Spangler's research group uses TRS to investigate optical materials and the mechanisms by which they function. These include laser, photorefractive, and optical-power-limiting materials, all three of which have complicated energy and charge transfer processes that occur after the initial photoexcitation. These processes can cause spectral changes anywhere in the ultraviolet to infrared range, and thus, they require a spectroscopic technique capable of yielding information in a relatively short experiment time—a need that TRS fulfills well. To investigate laser materials that have potential commercial uses, researchers must acquire the emission intensity as a function of time and, simultaneously, the emission frequency. In contrast, the desired information for optical-power-limiting materials is the change in absorption caused by the initial photoexcitation. So Spangler's group has developed Fourier transform techniques to acquire time-resolved, photoinduced absorption spectra on time scales from 10 ps to minutes.

TRS is ideal for dating inanimate materials whose ages cannot be determined using standard carbon-14 techniques, and so it fills an important technological gap. Ian Bailiff, an archeologist and one of Monkman's CTRS colleagues at the University of Durham, uses TRS for archeological dating of minerals and rocks. Such materials trap photons from the sun, which form new excited states inside minerals that can survive for thousands of years. Bailiff monitors the decay of the excitation states with TRS and thus, he can date rocks and minerals on the basis of the decay rate . . .

Future Challenges

Expanding the wavelength range for generated pulses ranks among the most desired improvements to existing TRS systems. Most lasers generate pulses in the ultraviolet to infrared range. Currently, however, a great deal of interest is focused on using the emerging area of terahertz radiation for TRS because that time scale yields specific characteristics from one material to another, according to Monkman. "Those who work with terahertz radiation say you can read a book with the cover closed, because you can see through the cover and observe the ink underneath," he says.

Such a development would make TRS useful for medical applications, particularly tomography and optical imaging, and help to continue the trend of making lasers smaller and more compact. In fact, Monkman envisions a day when spectroscopy will provide a simple detection system for biomolecules in a doctor's office. "It will also make our life much easier for doing true optical detection of biological systems," he adds, such as optical assays for analyzing biomolecules. TeraView Ltd. (Cambridge, England) is the first company to produce a commercially viable instrument for time-resolved terahertz spectroscopy.

Perhaps the greatest limiting factor to achieving ever-faster TRS time scales is the inherent limitations of the detectors. For example, in the FTIR step-scan method, going to faster time frames becomes possible only by making the detectors smaller—to the point where one could collect little light with them. This is not problematic for those using pump-probe techniques because a laser is an intrinsically bright source. But for the type of research conducted by Spangler and his Montana State colleagues, for example, researchers need to acquire a broad spectral range, which pump-probe techniques do not provide. The only possible source for high levels of intrinsic brightness in such applications is synchrotron beam lines, which are pulsed, like lasers, and ideal for TRS studies. Indeed, some scientists are actively engaged in such pursuits at facilities such as Brookhaven National

Laboratory, Lawrence Berkeley National Laboratory, and Duke University.

However, synchrotrons are expensive, and because so few exist, they represent a small niche market for companies interested in commercializing TRS. "In terms of an FTIR product for the general market, I don't see the time regimes getting any shorter in the foreseeable future," says Jackson. Even pump-probe spectroscopy is approaching its limitations as the laser pulses used become shorter and shorter. "With a much brighter source, we can use smaller detectors and reach shorter time scales, although it is difficult to envision what we could use as an intrinsically bright source in a general product. But the most fatal thing you can say is, 'It can never be done.'"

Reprinted with permission from "Time-Resolved Spectroscopy Comes of Age," by Ouellette, Jennifer, *The Industrial Physicist*, Feb./March 2004, Vol. 10, No. 1, pp. 16–19. © 2004, American Institute of Physics.

Sound Wave Applications

6

A sound wave is acoustic energy traveling along a rapidly varying series of compressions and rarefactions of the atoms or molecules that constitute the wave media. Any given atom alternates between participating in a compression, where the particles are pushed closer together, and participating in a rarefaction, where the particles are pushed apart. The pressure and temperature increase in the compressions and decrease in the rarefactions. This feature has allowed scientists to develop the thermoacoustic engine, a way to transport heat energy using acoustic waves as the "bucket brigade" carrying the energy. Physicists Steven L. Garrett, a professor in the graduate program in acoustics at Pennsylvania State University, and Scott Backhaus, at Los Alamos National Laboratory, explain the details of how the thermoacoustic engine accomplishes its task without needless pollution or wasteful mechanical complexity. —LCK

From "The Power of Sound"
by Steven L. Garrett and Scott Backhaus
American Scientist, **November/December 2000**

Last February, a panel of the National Academy of Engineering announced the results of its effort to rank the greatest engineering achievements of the 20th century. Second and tenth on that list were two very successful heat engines: the automobile (and hence, the internal-combustion engine) and the refrigerator and air conditioner, heat engines operated in reverse. But these two pillars of modern technology share another, less flattering distinction: Both have inadvertently damaged the environment by clouding skies with smog, spewing greenhouse gases or leaking compounds that erode the earth's protective blanket of stratospheric ozone.

Over the past two decades, investigators like ourselves have worked to develop an entirely new class of engines and refrigerators that may help reduce or eliminate such threats. These *thermoacoustic* devices produce or absorb sound power, rather than the "shaft power" characteristic of rotating machinery. Because of its inherent mechanical simplicity, such equipment may one day serve widely, perhaps generating electricity at individual homes, while producing domestic hot water and providing space heating or cooling.

How do these machines work? In a nutshell, a thermoacoustic engine converts heat from a high-temperature source into acoustic power while rejecting waste heat to a low-temperature sink. A thermoacoustic refrigerator does the opposite, using acoustic power to pump heat from a cool source to a hot sink. These devices perform best when they employ noble gases as their thermodynamic working fluids. Unlike the chemicals used in refrigeration over the years, such gases are both nontoxic and environmentally benign. Another appealing feature of thermoacoustics is that one can easily flange an engine onto a refrigerator, creating a heat-powered cooler with no moving parts at all.

So far, most machines of this variety reside in laboratories. But prototype thermoacoustic refrigerators have operated on the Space Shuttle and aboard a Navy warship. And a powerful thermoacoustic engine has recently demonstrated its ability to liquefy natural gas on a commercial scale . . .

Speech and Hot Air

The interaction of heat and sound has interested acousticians since 1816, when Laplace corrected Newton's earlier calculation of the speed of sound in air. Newton had assumed that the expansions and compressions of a sound wave in a gas happen without affecting the temperature. Laplace accounted for the slight variations in temperature that in fact take place, and by doing so he derived the correct speed of sound in air, a value that is 18 percent faster than Newton's estimate.

Such thermal effects also explain why 19th-century glassblowers occasionally heard their heated vessels emit pure tones—a hint that thermoacoustics might have some interesting practical consequences. Yet it took more than a century for anyone to recognize the opposite effect: Just as a temperature difference could create sound, sound could produce a temperature difference—hot to one side, cool to the other. How acoustic cooling can arise is, in retrospect, rather easy to understand.

Suppose an acoustic wave excites a gas that was initially at some average temperature and pressure. At any one spot, the temperature will go up as the pressure increases, assuming the rise happens rapidly enough that heat has no time to flow away. The change in temperature that accompanies the acoustic compressions depends on the magnitude of the pressure fluctuations. For ordinary speech, the relative pressure changes are on the order of only one part per million (equivalent to 74 decibels, or dB, in sound pressure levels), and the associated variation in temperature is a mere tenthousandth of a degree Celsius. Even for sounds at the auditory threshold of pain (120 dB), temperature oscillates up and down by only about 0.02 degree.

Most refrigerators and air conditioners must pump heat over considerably greater temperature ranges, usually 20 degrees or more. So the temperature swings that typical sound waves bring about are too small to be useful. To handle larger temperature spans, the gas must be put in contact with a solid material. Solids have much higher heat capacities per unit volume than gases, so they can exchange a considerable amount of heat without changing in temperature by very much. If a gas carrying a sound wave is placed near a solid surface, the solid will tend to absorb the heat of compression, keeping the temperature stable. The opposite is also true: The solid releases heat when the gas expands, preventing it from cooling down as much as it otherwise would.

The distance over which the diffusion of heat to or from an adjacent solid can take place is called the *thermal penetration depth*. Its value depends on the frequency of the passing sound wave and the properties of the gas. In typical thermoacoustic devices, and for sound waves in air at audio frequencies, the thermal penetration depth is typically on the order of one-tenth of a millimeter. So to optimize the exchange of heat, the design of a thermoacoustic engine or refrigerator must include a solid with gaps that are about twice this dimension in width, through which a high-amplitude sound wave propagates. The porous solid (frequently a jelly-roll of plastic for refrigerators or of stainless steel for engines), is called a "stack," because it contains many layers and thus resembles a stack of plates.

When an acoustically driven gas moves through the stack, pressure, temperature and position all oscillate with time. If the gas is enclosed within a tube, sound bounces back and forth creating an acoustic standing wave. In that case, pressure will be in phase with displacement—that is, the pressure reaches its maximum or minimum value when the gas is at an extreme of its oscillatory motion.

Consider how this simple relation can be put to use in a thermoacoustic refrigerator, which in its most rudimentary form amounts to a closed tube, a porous stack and a source of acoustic energy. As a parcel of gas moves to one side, say to the left, it heats up as the pressure rises and then comes momentarily to rest

Figure 2

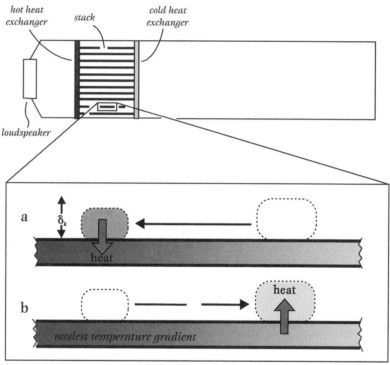

refrigerator

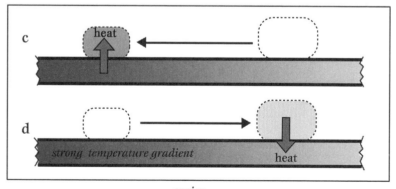

engine

Figure 2. Thermoacoustic device consists, in essence, of a gas-filled tube containing a "stack" *(top)*, a porous solid with many open channels through which the gas can pass. Resonating sound waves (created, for example, by a loudspeaker) force gas to move back and forth through openings in the stack. If the temperature gradient along the stack is modest *(middle)*, gas shifted to one side *(a)* will be compressed and warmed so that a parcel of gas with dimensions that are roughly equal to the thermal penetration depth (δ_k) releases heat to the stack. When this same gas then shifts in the other direction *(b)*, it expands and cools enough to absorb heat. Although an individual parcel carries heat just a small distance, the many parcels making up the gas form a "bucket brigade," which transfers heat from a cold region to a warm one and thus provides refrigeration. The same device can be turned into a thermoacoustic engine *(bottom)* if the temperature difference along the stack is made sufficiently large. In that case, sound can also compress and warm a parcel of gas *(c)*, but it remains cooler than the stack and thus absorbs heat. When this gas shifts to the other side and expands *(d)*, it cools but stays hotter than the stack and thus releases heat. Hence, the parcel thermally expands at high pressure and contracts at low pressure, which amplifies the pressure oscillations of the reverberating sound waves, transforming heat energy into acoustic energy.

before reversing direction. Near the end of its motion, the hot gas deposits heat into the stack, which is somewhat cooler. During the next half-cycle, the parcel of gas moves to the right and expands. When it reaches its rightmost extreme, it will be colder than the adjacent portion of the stack and will extract heat from it. The result is that the parcel pumps heat from right to left and can do so even when the left side of the stack is hotter than the right.

The span of movement for an individual parcel is quite small, but the net effect is that of a bucket brigade: Each parcel of oscillating gas takes heat from the one behind and hands this heat off to the next one ahead. The heat, plus the work done to move it thermoacoustically exits one end of the stack through a hot heat exchanger (similar to a car radiator). A cold heat exchanger, located at the other end of the stack, provides useful cooling to some external heat load.

One can easily reverse this process of refrigeration to make a thermoacoustic engine. Just apply heat at the hot end of the stack and remove it at the cold end, creating a steep temperature gradient. Now when a parcel of gas moves to the left, its pressure and temperature rise as before, but the stack at that point is hotter still. So heat flows from the stack into the gas, causing it to expand thermally just as pressure reaches a maximum. Conversely, when the parcel shifts to the right, it expands and cools, but the stack there is cooler still. So heat flows into the solid from the gas, causing thermal contraction just as pressure reaches a minimum. In this way, the temperature variation imposed on the stack drives heat into and out of the gas, forcing it to do work on its surroundings and amplifying the acoustic oscillations. Maintenance of the steep thermal gradient requires an external source of power, such as an electric heater, concentrated sunlight or a flame—which explains why glassblowers sometimes observe the spontaneous generation of sound when they heat the walls of a glass tube (serving as a stack) in such a way as to create a strong temperature gradient, a phenomenon first documented in a scholarly journal in 1850 . . .

One of the most remarkable features of such thermoacoustic engines is that they have no moving parts.

They demand nothing beyond the basic physics of the cavity and stack to force the compressions, expansions, displacements and heat transfers to happen at the right times. The internal-combustion engines in our cars also depend on proper timing—the intake, compression, expansion and exhaust stages of the power cycle must take place in smooth succession. But conventional automobile engines require at least two valves per cylinder, each with a spring, rocker arm and a push rod (or an overhead cam driven by a timing belt) to produce the required phasing. This difference makes thermoacoustic devices much simpler and potentially much more reliable than conventional engines and refrigerators, because they can avoid wear associated with valves, piston rings, crankshafts, connecting rods and so forth. Thus thermoacoustic devices require no lubrication . . .

The Next Competition

Thermoacoustic engines and refrigerators were already being considered a few years ago for specialized applications, where their simplicity, lack of lubrication and sliding seals, and their use of environmentally harmless working fluids were adequate compensation for their lower efficiencies. This latest breakthrough, coupled with other developments in the design of highpower, single-frequency loudspeakers and reciprocating electric generators, suggests that thermoacoustics may soon emerge as an environmentally attractive way to power hybrid electric vehicles, capture solar energy, refrigerate food, air condition buildings, liquefy industrial gases and serve in other capacities that are yet to be imagined.

In 2099, the National Academy of Engineering probably will again convene an expert panel to select the outstanding technological achievements of the 21st century. We hope the machines that our unborn grandchildren see on that list will include thermoacoustic devices, which promise to improve everyone's standard of living while helping to protect the planet. We and a small band of interested physicists and engineers have been working hard over the past two decades to make acoustic engines and refrigerators part of that future. The latest achievements are certainly encouraging, but there is still much left to be done.

Reprinted with permission from Dr. Steven Garrett.

Optical microscopes are common tools in every laboratory, and everyone knows you peer into a microscope with your eye. So the idea of an acoustic microscope, listening with your ears perhaps, seems silly. But acoustic microscopes are becoming important laboratory tools on their own, using sound to measure the elastic properties of materials and finding applications in materials failure analysis, biology, and diagnostic medicine, for example. You don't listen with your ears; the sound is collected by piezoelectric detectors that are sensitive to the variations in a sound pressure wave, then transformed into visual images electronically.

Science writer Jennifer Ouellette describes how replacing light waves with sound waves, and replacing the optical lens with an acoustic lens, has opened up for examination materials and subjects, such as living biological tissue, that could not be observed before. —LCK

From "Seeing with Sound"
by Jennifer Ouellette
Industrial Physicist, June/July 2004

About 5,000 years ago in ancient Assyria, scribes recorded on clay tablets the existence of magical magnifying stones that made objects seem larger. These stones were actually broken shards of meteorites whose centers had fused into glass during the intense heat of entry into Earth's atmosphere, melting it in such away that they formed a primitive lens. Although the Assyrians did not know it, they were practicing the earliest known optical microscopy, a technology that has unequivocally revolutionized almost every aspect of science. Now its cousin, acoustic microscopy, is making inroads into areas such as materials characterization, biology, and medical diagnosis, and giving researchers yet another valuable tool in their imaging arsenal.

Acoustic microscopy essentially replaces light waves with sound waves. Whereas optical microscopy provides an image of the optical (or electrical) properties of a material, acoustic microscopy provides an image of the acoustic (or elastic) properties. Russian physicist Sergei Y. Sokolov first proposed the concept in 1928, but it took another 40 years before computer and ultrasound technologies became sufficiently developed to enable the building of practical instruments. Two separate systems emerged in the1970s: one at Zenith Laboratories in Chicago, and another at Stanford University. Since then, more-advanced systems have entered the marketplace, but the basic design has remained much the same.

Sound Qualities

In acoustic microscopy, the familiar optical lens is replaced by an acoustic lens, which serves the same function but redirects sound waves rather than light. A sound wave is sent through a piece of quartz or glass coated with a thin layer of piezoelectric material that resonates at a specific frequency—for example, 1 GHz. The bottom of the glass lens is hollowed into a bowl shape to form an inverted, or concave, lens. The sound waves are reflected to the edge of the lens, and then they pass through a film of water on a glass slide, which focuses them for scanning over a sample's surface. The waves are then reflected back up through the lens and piezoelectric crystal, which serve as a detector and amplifier. The sound waves are recorded electronically and then translated into an image on a video monitor.

An acoustic microscope's ability to provide information about the mechanical properties of a sample makes it a valuable tool, particularly for materials and biomedical uses, notes Joie Jones, a professor of radiology at the University of California, Irvine. "It gives you an entirely new dimension of information about a tissue sample or material," he says. "Acoustic microscopy enables you to see subtleties in materials that you just cannot see with conventional optical microscopy." As an example, Jones points to small, stressed areas in materials that are prone to breakage—defects often missed by optical methods. Because the sound wave is a mechanical wave, it can interact with a material's elastic properties.

Acoustic microscopy has its limitations, mostly stemming from the differences in the physical properties of light waves compared with sound waves. The wavelength or frequency of the light used in any optical microscopy system ultimately determines the resolution capabilities of the instrument. This is also true of acoustic microscopy. With visible light, resolution is limited to about 0.5 μm, with a magnification of about 2,000 times. The human ear is capable of hearing sounds only in a limited range of frequencies, between 20 and 20,000 Hz. These frequencies have much longer wavelengths than light, so to build an acoustic microscope with resolution on a par with optical instruments, scientists must use ultrasonic sound waves with frequencies of around 1 GHz.

Failure Analysis

This is, perhaps, one reason why acoustic microscopy has tended to remain a niche technology. Its primary application to date has been for failure analysis in the multibillion-dollar microelectronics industry. The technique is especially sensitive to variations in the elastic properties of semiconductor materials, such as air gaps, known as delaminations or voids, according to Larry

Kessler, president of Sonoscan (Elk Grove Village, IL). Acoustic microscopy enables nondestructive internal inspection of plastic integrated-circuit (IC) packages, and, more recently, it has provided a tool for characterizing packaging processes such as die attachment and encapsulation. Even as ICs continue to shrink, their die size becomes larger because of added functionality; in fact, devices measuring as much as 1 cm across are now common. And as die sizes increase, cracks and delaminations become more likely at the various interfaces . . .

IBM, Motorola, and Hewlett-Packard are among the manufacturers who use acoustic microscopy as part of their failure-analysis procedure. The technique weeds out electrical failures caused by bent, missing, or dirty leads. It also can help engineers identify root causes of device failures related to stress on IC packaging materials and its correlation to device electrical malfunctions. Ralph Carbone of Hewlett-Packard reports that, in the company's experience, if acoustic imaging reveals a crack, void, or other gap defect in a component package, physical cross-sectioning will ultimately show the same defect in that same location. But physical sectioning takes hours and destroys the component, and if the defect is missed, it may not be possible to section the component again. Acoustic microscopy requires no special preparation of the component package and takes only about 15 s. In fact, Hewlett-Packard's failure-analysis laboratory in Roseville, California, has largely abandoned physical cross-sectioning and now relies primarily on acoustic microscopy and an occasional X-ray analysis.

Materials Characterization

A related, more research-oriented application of acoustic microscopy lies in materials characterization. Ken Telschow and his colleagues at the Idaho National Engineering and Environmental Laboratory use lasers to generate and detect sound waves in an acoustic microscope. For example, to image a microelectronic circuit, a pulsed or chopped laser beam heats a localized region of the sample about 10 μm in diameter, while a second green laser beam detects the ultrasonic motion of the local surface using an interferometer. Thus, Rayleigh surface waves and longitudinal bulk waves can be observed traveling through the circuit, which allows making measurements of properties such as film thickness, substrate bonding, and substrate flaws. The source laser can be focused to 1–2 μm and can generate and detect frequencies of about 1 GHz. This is important because at gigahertz frequencies, the acoustic wavelengths are on the order of a few micrometers, with corresponding resolution.

Telschow and his colleagues use the instrument to study ultrasonic wave propagation in material microstructures at the individual-grain level. "Materials fail because of things that are happening at the single-grain level," he says. As materials bend back and forth, the stress causes dislocations to occur—not quite a fracture, just a small change in the crystalline structure. However, such dislocations tend to multiply and eventually create a tiny crack in the material, usually at grain boundaries. Ideally, materials scientists would like to construct materials that can be subjected to a great deal of stress and fatigue without cracking.

"We're down to resolutions where every grain is like a small crystal, and we know very well how acoustic waves act in crystals," Telschow says. "So we can measure and predict the properties of the acoustic waves as they go from one crystal to another." By modeling that entire process, Telschow hopes to develop an acoustic model of sound-wave propagation at the micrometer scale, which would make acoustics more useful for measuring materials' microstructural properties. Being able to map what he terms a material's "road to failure" would enable researchers and non-destructive testing engineers to tell when a material is likely to fail, thereby extending the service lifetime of materials.

Biological Uses

Only a few research groups to date have applied acoustic microscopy to biology and diagnostic medicine. "For some reason, the technique has never gotten the attention I think it deserves," says Jones, whose work in the field dates back to its infancy in the 1970s. "I thought it would play a major role in biomedicine, and I have been proven wrong." Despite this, Jones believes that biomedical applications could become a major growth area for the technology. Many biological materials have a wider range of values for their elastic properties— which vary as much as 2 orders of magnitude—than for their optical properties, whose variation is only 0.5 %. Thus, optical microscopes have a limited contrast capability. Specimens must be prepared with appropriate stains designed to bring out particular features of the sample, such as specific pathologies or biochemical processes. Acoustic microscopy, however, provides a sensitive tool for imaging soft-tissue structures without the need for staining or elaborate sample preparation.

Acoustic microscopy could provide an immediate assessment of pathology long before conventional methods, according to Jones. For example, applying a special ultrasound scanner directly to the skin of a patient could provide real-time microscopy, and pathological assessments of skin tumors or lesions could be made noninvasively. Jones is developing such an acoustic instrumentation for virtual biopsies and mapping the configuration and extent of tumors prior to surgery. He has also used the technique to study acupuncture points in the body—particularly what happens in response to stimulation by needles—and he has observed the mechanical responses of these points using a 100-MHz acoustic microscope. He found that the nerves that form the points twist themselves around an inserted needle, which may explain the tactile sensation known among acupuncturists as stickiness.

Although the resolution of acoustical microscopy is currently limited to the cellular rather than the molecular level—the maximum resolution is about 0.1 μm—the technique can still provide uniquely useful information on the mechanical properties of biological tissues, such as Alzheimer's plaques. Acoustic microscopy is already advancing cardiology, specifically in the area of intravascular ultrasound (IVUS), in which physicians are able to thread a small ultrasound device into the body to examine artery blockage.

Scientists at Tohoku University in Japan, for example, are using a scanning acoustic microscope for IVUS to gather basic data on the fatty deposits or arterial plaques that cause atherosclerosis, a condition difficult to study in vivo. Atherosclerosis contributes to heart attacks and strokes that kill about 640,000 U.S. residents annually, according to the American Heart Association.

In The Netherlands, Ton van der Steen and his colleagues at the Erasmus Medical Center (Rotterdam) have developed a clinical technique called IVUS elasticity imaging, which can detect the arterial plaques most likely to rupture and cause a heart attack or stroke. The technique measures the local deformation of athero- sclerosis caused by variations in blood pressure. It does this by using the phase information of high-frequency ultrasound. According to van der Steen, high deformation (or strain) indicates the presence of a lipid deposit covered by a thin fibrous (and usually inflamed) cap. Caps weakened by inflammation may break apart and release pieces of debris that can lead to athrombosis, causing a stroke or heart attack. The primary drawback of the technique is that several sets of data must be taken and analyzed to make an accurate diagnosis. The Erasmus researchers are currently focusing on finding ways to eliminate the number of false positives that result from the instrument detecting high-strain spots that are not plaques vulnerable to rupture but are caused by other phenomena.

Finally, acoustic microscopy of cells or tissue in culture enables scientists to examine living structures without killing them, as happens using optical means. Tissue requires the use of light at extremely high frequencies to obtain adequate resolution, which in turn damages or destroys the cells. "Biologists could put cells growing in a petri dish under an acoustic microscope and image those cells continuously in real time," Jones says. "You could study the cells as they grow and develop, and learn a great deal about cell structure in the process."

In this short article, a team of scientists from the French National Institute for Health and Medical Research (INSERM), led by Cyril Lafon, brings to our attention an important advancement in the use of ultrasound for the removal of tumors in the human body. Ultrasound is high-frequency sound, too high in pitch for humans to hear. But even though our hearing does not detect such sound, biological materials do respond to ultrasound, such as when high-intensity focused ultrasound (HIFU) is used to heat up a tumor to destroy it. The article describes how taking HIFU inside the body with special plane wave sources can precisely reach buried tumors without heating up intervening tissue, providing a safe, bloodless cancer treatment. —LCK

"Destroying Deep-Seated Tumors with 'Interstitial' Ultrasound"
by Cyril Lafon, David Melodelima, Jean-Yves Chapelon, and Dominique Cathignol
Paper presented at the 147th Acoustical Society of America Meeting, New York, NY, May 25, 2004

High Intensity Focused Ultrasound (HIFU) is now an accepted therapeutic method for removing tumors. In this approach, intense ultrasound waves focus inside the body to heat up a tumor and coagulate it. This process of intense heating is known as "thermal ablation" and several devices for carrying out this task are currently marketed. This method of destroying tumors is non-invasive when using ultrasound sources that are "extracorporeal," or originate from outside the body.

However, extracorporeal HIFU is not always suitable for treating some tumors, such as ones that are deeply buried or "deep seated." Moreover, intervening tissue between the ultrasound device and the tumor may contain bones or gaseous pockets, in which the ultrasound wave cannot propagate. While traveling through tissue, an ultrasound wave is naturally attenuated (weakened) and deformed (e.g., phase-aberrated) in structures with different geometric and acoustic properties. Attenuation or phase aberration during treatment of deep-seated tumors results in a decrease in the amount of sound pressure that can be delivered to destroy a tumor. In this case, sound pressure can be increased at the surface of the ultrasound-generating device in the hope of supplying sufficient energy to the point inside the body where the ultrasound focuses (*i.e.*, the tumor). However, this increase is to the detriment of intervening tissue whose temperature will also rise.

Therefore, we have developed a new minimally invasive approach, one that uses a device known as an "interstitial applicator," which brings the ultrasound source into contact with the target via natural routes in order to minimize the effects of attenuation and phase aberration. It then becomes possible to use higher ultrasound frequencies, which increases the absorption of ultrasound in the desired area and thereby leads to a more efficient heating of the treatment region. In contrast to extracorporeal applicators, interstitial probes impose additional design constraints with regard to size and ergonomics.

In this paper, the technological and clinical research carried out by Unit 556 of the French National Institute for Health and Medical Research (INSERM) over the last years will be presented. Our research aims to develop ultrasound endoscopic applicators for treating cancers of the esophagus and the biliary duct. Systemic treatments such as radiotherapy are not effective on these digestive cancers. Surgery is the only curative treatment available but very few patients are able to undergo this surgery because of their general condition and the late diagnosis of these tumors. Prognosis is extremely poor and only palliative care (placing of prostheses) can be undertaken. These tumors develop locally around the lumens (spaces) in the biliary or esophageal organs and are therefore good candidates for local treatment by intraluminal thermotherapy (Figure 1).

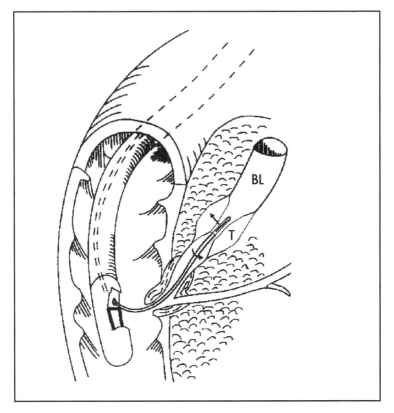

Figure 1. Endoscopic application of high intensity ultrasound on tumors (T) in the biliary lumen (BL). The applicator is brought into contact with the tumor.

The technique uses non-focalized plane transducers, ultrasound generators that do not focus ultrasound to tiny points but instead produce "plane waves," sound waves whose fronts form flat parallel planes. The transducer destroys tumors through the process of coagulation necrosis, in which heated tumor cells agglomerate into a lifeless mass. To compensate for the absence of focalization, it is necessary to operate the transducer at a high frequency (10 MHz). The treatment depth is directly related to the ultrasound frequency. The higher the frequency, the less the ultrasound penetrates the tissue, and the more intense the heat. Even when coagulating cylindrical volumes of tissue are required for covering the total volume of the tumor, a rotating transducer is preferred to a tubular transducer. Indeed, the divergence of acoustical waves associated with tubular transducers results in a rapid fall in sound pressure that limits the depth and/or increases the duration of treatment. In order to minimize the movement of the applicator, we have developed an ultrasound cylindrical phased array composed of 64 elements for transesophageal thermal ablation. Based on the principal of dynamic focalization, the 64 small transducers mounted on a tubular frame are excited successively. Depending on the delay times of the excitation of each element, a plane wave can be generated with a group of elements (Figure 2). Rotation of the plane wave is obtained by exciting a group of neighboring transducers. Depending on the application, different guiding methods were tested: ultrasound, MRI and fluoroscopy. The interest of MRI lies in the fact that this imaging modality can give in almost real time temperature monitoring whilst controlling the extent of coagulation necrosis. However, it requires constructing non-magnetic applicators that do not induce artifacts on the image.

A pilot study was carried out in 10 patients who were diagnosed with cholangiocarcinoma, malignant tumors in the biliary duct system. The applicator

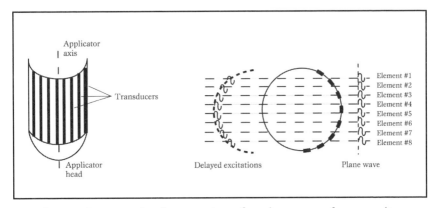

Figure 2. Principle of generation of a plane wave from a cylindrical array.

used was compatible with conventional gastrointestinal endoscopic equipment. A guide wire enabled the applicator to exit the endoscope and move up into the biliary ducts to the tumor. The method is minimally invasive since the duration of anesthesia was not significantly prolonged and both the treatment and the control examinations corresponded to the dates when prostheses (such as stents which keep the biliary duct open) needed to be renewed. For some patients, who underwent surgery after ultrasound treatment, analysis of the removed tumor demonstrated 10 mm deep coagulation necrosis at the targeted point. In most cases, local tumor regression was observed with proliferation in the distal end (farther from the center of the body) resulting from a pre-treatment under-estimate of tumor spread. In one case, the tumor was completely destroyed and bile flow restored. Future studies should determine whether this endoscopic ultrasound treatment of biliary tumors is a new palliative method (one that relieves symptoms but does not eliminate the disease) or whether it could be curative in high-risk surgery patients exhibiting localized tumors.

Conclusion:

When used with modern imaging modalities, interstitial therapeutic ultrasound devices offer very promising options for cancer treatment. These methods are suitable for treating deep-seated tumors, and are precise, safe, repeatable, bloodless and economic.

7 Electromagnetic Wave Applications

The air is filled with electromagnetic waves. All the radio and television station signals and the signals being sent and received by countless cellular phones surround us in an invisible sea of waves. Some of this is unavoidable; each radio station needs to have its signal present just in case you turn on your radio to that station. But why is the cellular phone signal from Joe B. Citizen wafting around your room? It is unlikely that Joe is going to walk into the millions of rooms where his signal waits for him; he will answer the call only in the one specific location where he happens to be at this moment. There are thousands of other unnecessary signals broadcast in all directions by the cellular networks as well. Martin Cooper, a cofounder of a company that produces "smart antennas" (antenna arrays that communicate with powerful digital processors), tells how the wasted energy and unwanted electromagnetic interference and pollution this situation produces can be avoided by using arrays of antennas to project cellular phone and other signals. Such *adaptive antenna arrays can pinpoint the source of a radio signal and selectively amplify it while ignoring other unwanted signals, a feat that promises to improve the capacity for data transmission of cellular base stations many times over their present capacity. —LCK*

From "Antennas Get Smart"
by Martin Cooper
Scientific American, **July 2003**

Each of us is immersed in a sea of radio-frequency waves. The invisible electromagnetic energy comes from many sources: broadcast towers, cellular-phone networks and police radio transmissions, among others. Although this radiation may be harmless to our bodies, it can severely inhibit our ability to receive and transmit information. Excess radio energy is a kind of pollution, because it can disrupt useful communications. As the intensity of radio-frequency interference in our environment grows, we have to raise the volume of radio signals so that they can be heard over the electromagnetic background noise. And as our electronic communications become more intense, they simply add to the din of radio interference.

One solution to this problem lies in a new class of radio antennas that could dramatically reduce man-made interference. Instead of wastefully broadcasting personal communications—such as cell-phone calls—in all directions, these innovative antennas track the positions of mobile users and deliver radio signals directly to them. These antenna systems also maximize the reception of

an individual cell-phone user's signal while minimizing the interference from other users. In effect, the antennas create a virtual wire extending to each mobile phone.

These systems are generically referred to as smart antennas, but the smartest members of the class are called adaptive antenna arrays. In 1992 I co-founded ArrayComm, a San Jose, Calif., company focused on developing adaptive arrays that can be incorporated into both new and existing wireless networks. Each of our arrays consists of up to a dozen antennas and a powerful digital processor that can combine and manipulate the incoming and outgoing signals. The technology, which is also being pursued by Lucent Technologies, Nortel Networks and other firms, promises to decrease the cost and improve the quality of wireless communications. Adaptive antenna arrays are already providing these benefits to millions of cell-phone users. Moreover, these smart antennas may become the linchpins of the wireless Internet because they are ideally suited to transmitting and receiving large amounts of data.

The Physics of Antennas

To understand how smart antennas operate, it helps to know how ordinary, "dumb" antennas work. A radio antenna converts electric currents and voltages created by a transmitter into electromagnetic waves that radiate into space. Antennas also intercept such waves and convert them back into currents and voltages that can be processed by a receiver. The simplest and most common radio antennas, called dipoles, are merely rods of very specific lengths that radiate energy in all directions [see top illustration on page 154]. Radio waves get weaker as they spread through space and are absorbed by obstacles such as air, trees and buildings.

Commercial radio and television stations need to reach geographically dispersed audiences, so it is logical for them to broadcast signals in all directions. A cell-phone call, though, is usually aimed at just one user. In a cellular network, users communicate with the nearest base station, a set of antennas that handle all the wireless service's signals in the surrounding area (called the cell). The base stations are located so that the entire coverage area can be divided into cells; when a user moves from one cell to another, the system automatically hands off the call to the appropriate base station. In this situation, it would be far preferable to focus the radio energy on each user, much as the reflector in a flashlight focuses light into a beam. A radio beam would extend much farther than a signal of equivalent power that is broadcast in all directions. And because the radio beams transmitted by the cellular base station to different users would be spatially separated, interference would be reduced.

Reflectors can focus radio waves into beams, but they are cumbersome and costly. So engineers have developed tricks to create radio beams without reflectors. If we stand two antennas side by side, with the distance between them equal to one half the wavelength of the radio signal, the radiated energy from this simple array assumes the pattern of a figure eight when viewed from above [see middle illustration on page 154]. The radio waves travel farthest in the two directions perpendicular to the array (that is, perpendicular to the line connecting

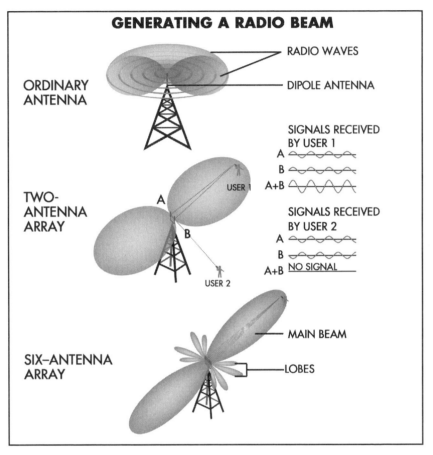

GENERATING A RADIO BEAM

ORDINARY ANTENNA

RADIO WAVES

DIPOLE ANTENNA

TWO-ANTENNA ARRAY

USER 1

A

B

USER 2

SIGNALS RECEIVED BY USER 1

A

B

A+B

SIGNALS RECEIVED BY USER 2

A

B

A+B NO SIGNAL

SIX–ANTENNA ARRAY

MAIN BEAM

LOBES

the antennas), because in these directions the user would receive both antenna signals at the exact same time (in other words, the two signals would be in phase). When two identical signals are in phase, they combine to form a signal that is twice as strong as either one alone. But in the directions parallel to the array, the user would receive the two antenna signals 180 degrees out of phase. The wave peaks from one antenna would arrive at the same time as the wave troughs from the other, so the two signals would cancel each other out. This phenomenon creates a null, an area where the signal cannot be detected.

The beam generated by the two-antenna array is a fairly broad one, and it extends in opposite directions. But engineers can progressively narrow the beam by adding more antennas. Such phased-array antennas have been used to focus radar beams since World War II. Although increasing the number of antennas makes the beam narrower, it also produces smaller beams, called lobes, on both sides of the main beam [see bottom illustration on page 154]. Depending on the user's direction from the antenna array, the signal can be either stronger than the signal radiated by a single antenna ("gain") or weaker because of cancellation effects ("rejection") . . .

The Cocktail Party Effect

What makes the adaptive array so smart? The key step is processing the information received by its antennas. A good analogy is the way the brain processes acoustic information from the ears. A person with normal hearing can usually locate the source of a sound even with his or her eyes closed. The convoluted folds of the outer ear produce differing resonances depending on the angle of the incoming sound. And unless the sound is coming from directly ahead or behind (or directly above or below), it reaches one ear before the other, so there is a time lag between the two signals. The brain receives this information and rapidly computes the location of the source.

What is more, people with normal hearing can pick up relatively quiet sounds—say, an interesting conversation—amid loud background noise. This phenomenon is commonly known as the cocktail party effect. Researchers have shown that the ability to focus on a specific sound partly depends on the ability to locate the sound's source. In an experiment that tested how well people can hear a signal while being blasted with background noise, subjects listening with both ears were able to detect much softer sounds than subjects listening with only one ear. Once the brain has determined the position of the acoustic source, it can focus on the sound and tune out unwanted noise coming from other directions.

Similarly, an adaptive antenna array can pinpoint the source of a radio signal and selectively amplify it while canceling out competing signals. The array's brain is a digital processor that can manipulate the signals coming down the wires from the antennas. A typical adaptive array contains four to 12 antennas, but for simplicity's sake let us consider an array of two antennas, separated by a distance equal to half the wavelength of the radio signal. In an ordinary array the signals from the two antennas are just added together, but in an adaptive array the signals are sent to the adjoining processor, which can perform any number of mathematical operations on them . . .

Benefits and Applications

Wireless networks that employ adaptive antenna arrays have several advantages over conventional cellular networks. Because a base station equipped with an adaptive array has a far greater range than an ordinary station transmitting at the same power, fewer stations are needed to cover a given area. Although adaptive arrays may be more expensive than traditional antennas, reducing the number of base stations dramatically cuts the overall cost of deploying and operating a wireless network.

Adaptive arrays also enable a cellular service company to make better use of a scarce resource: the spectrum of frequencies allotted to the company for its radio signals. Many cellular systems are becoming overloaded with customers—in certain congested sectors, the barrage of signals sometimes exceeds the amount that can be carried on the limited number of radio channels. Customers feel the crunch when their calls are dropped or they hear poor-quality signals. But because adaptive arrays allow several cell-phone users within a base station's coverage area to share the same radio channel, the technology increases the capacity of the spectrum. The improvement over ordinary antennas is significant: base stations outfitted with adaptive arrays can serve about six times as many people for voice communications and up to 40 times as many for data transmission. The result is better service and less interference, not to mention less wasted energy and radio pollution . . .

Adaptive arrays are also a boon to wireless data networks. Because the arrays minimize interference, they can receive and transmit more data to users in a given chunk of frequency spectrum. A base station equipped with an adaptive array could deliver data to as many as 40 concurrent users at a rate of one megabit a second, which is about 20 times as fast as the typical data rate for existing long-range wireless networks. Because all the users in such a network do not usually require peak data rates at the same time, one station with an adaptive array could serve several thousand people. Users with laptops or other portable devices would be able to get uninterrupted high-speed access to the Internet while walking or driving across the coverage area . . .

For almost 100 years after Alexander Graham Bell invented the telephone, voice communications relied on a physical connection—a copper wire or a coaxial cable—between the caller and the network. Over the past 30 years, though, cellular phones have given us a taste of the freedom to communicate without wires. With the help of adaptive-array technology, wireless carriers will be able to offer far better performance, at a much lower cost, than wired networks do. Only then will we rid ourselves of the copper cage.

Electromagnetic radiation ranges in wavelength from the infinitesimally small waves of gamma radiation to the very long radio waves. The interaction of solid and biological materials with the different regions of the electromagnetic spectrum has been studied to varying degrees, depending on the availability of the radiation source. Somewhere in between is a region of electromagnetic radiation that has been neglected because it has been difficult to make a source of such radiation. This is "terahertz" radiation, with wavelengths ranging from 30 µm

to 1 mm, just the right size to extensively interact with various forms of matter. In this excerpt, engineer Eric R. Mueller reports on new advances in terahertz source development, advances that will make accessible many new applications for different fields in biology, astronomy, physics, and engineering. —LCK

From "Terahertz Radiation: Applications and Sources"
by Eric R. Mueller
Industrial Physicist, August/September 2003

Until recently, researchers did not extensively explore the material interactions occurring in the terahertz spectral region—the wavelengths that lie between 30 μm and 1 mm—in part because they lacked reliable sources of terahertz radiation. However, pressure to develop new terahertz sources arose from two dramatically different groups—ultrafast time-domain spectroscopists who wanted to work with longer wavelengths, and long wavelength radio astronomers who wanted to work with shorter wavelengths. Today, with continuous-wave (CW) and pulsed sources readily available, investigators are pursuing potential terahertz-wavelength applications in many fields.

Bio and Astro

Much of the recent interest in terahertz radiation stems from its ability to penetrate deep into many organic materials without the damage associated with ionizing radiation such as X-rays (albeit without the spatial resolution). Also, because terahertz radiation is readily absorbed by water, it can be used to distinguish between materials with varying water content—for example, fat versus lean meat. These properties lend themselves to applications in process and quality control as well as biomedical imaging. Tests are currently under way to determine whether terahertz tomographic imaging can augment or replace mammography, and some people have proposed terahertz imaging as a method of screening passengers for explosives at airports. All of these applications are still in the research phase, although TeraView (Cambridge, England), which is partially owned by Toshiba, has developed a technique for detecting the presence of cancerous cells that is currently in human trials.

Terahertz radiation can also help scientists understand the complex dynamics involved in condensed-matter physics and processes such as molecular recognition and protein folding.

CW terahertz technology has long interested astronomers because "approximately one-half of the total luminosity and 98% of the photons emitted since the Big Bang fall into the submillimeter and far-infrared," says Peter Siegel of the Jet Propulsion Laboratory (Pasadena, CA), and CW THz sources can be used to help study these photons.

One type of CW terahertz source is the optically pumped terahertz laser (OPTL). OPTL lasers are in use around the world, primarily for astronomy, environ-mental monitoring, and plasma diagnostics. A system installed at the Antarctic Submillimeter Telescope and Remote Observatory at the South Pole is the local oscillator for a THz receiver, which will be used to measure interstellar singly ionized nitrogen, H_2D^+, and carbon monoxide during the polar winter. Another system is slated for sub-Doppler terahertz astronomy use on the National Aeronautics and Space Administration's SOFIA airborne astronomical platform.

In [July] 2004, a 2.5-THz laser [rode] a Delta rocket into space aboard NASA's AURA satellite to measure the concentration and distribution of the hydroxyl radical (OH^-) in the stratosphere, a critical component in the ozone cycle. (Currently there are no global data for OH^- concentrations; only two spot measurements have been made using OPTL systems carried aboard high-altitude balloons.) The AURA system is less than 0.2 m³, weighs less than 22 kg, and consumes 120 W of prime power. It works autonomously and is designed to operate [continuously, orbiting the earth once every 98 minutes,] for more than five years.

The emerging field of time domain spectroscopy (TDS) typically relies on a broadband short-pulse terahertz source. A split antenna is fabricated on a semiconductor substrate to create a switch. A dc bias is placed across the antenna, and an ultrashort pump-laser pulse (< 100 fs) is focused in the gap in the antenna. The bias-laser pulse combination allows electrons to rapidly jump the gap, and the resulting current in the antenna produces a terahertz electromagnetic wave. This radiation is collected and collimated with an appropriate optical system to produce a beam.

This TDS switch puts out a train of pulses, whose repetition frequency is the same as that of the femto-second pump laser. Pulse widths are on the order of 100 fs, with average powers of a few microwatts and a frequency spread of > 500 GHz. The pulse bandwidth is typically centered at about 1 to 2 THz. The details of the spectrum can vary significantly, however, depending on the design of the switch and pump-laser power, pulse width, and configuration.

Figure 2a shows a typical TDS setup. The terahertz pulse is distorted by selective absorption as it passes through a sample, causing delays in its arrival time at the detector. The transmitted beam is then focused onto a detector, which is essentially identical to the emitter except that it is unbiased. By varying the time at which the sample pump pulse arrives at the detector, successive portions of the terahertz pulses can be detected and built into a complete image of the pulse in terms of its delay time, or time domain. The data are then processed by fast Fourier transform analysis in order to convert the delay time into the frequency of the terahertz signal that arrives at the detector.

The absorption characteristics of terahertz radiation vary greatly from material to material, and this property can be used to create images. In 1995, Binbin Hu and Martin Nuss at Lucent Technologies' Bell Laboratories created a terahertz imaging system using TDS and coined the term T-ray for these short, broadband terahertz pulses. The T-ray pulse is measured as it reflects from a sample. Because the pulse is so short, distance can be resolved by looking at the time of flight and then used to create a three-dimensional transparent reconstruction of various objects by measuring the time lapse between pulses reflected from different areas within the object.

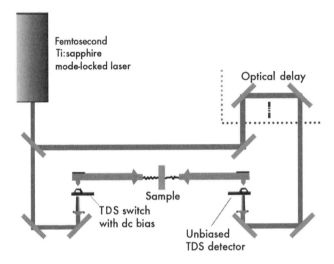

Figure 2. In time domain spectroscopy, an image of the sample is built up based on selective absorption, which causes delays in arrival time at the detector.

Optically Pumped Lasers

In its simplest embodiment, an OPTL system consists of a grating-tuned carbon dioxide pump laser and a far-infrared (FIR) gas cell mounted in a laser resonator. The pump beam enters the cell through an aperture in the high-reflecting resonator mirror. The pump laser is tuned to the appropriate absorption band, and lasing occurs. For several reasons, this is not as easy as it sounds. Both the absorption bandwidth of the vibrational energy state and the lasing bandwidth of its excited rotational states are quite narrow. Moreover, slight changes in the OPTL's pumping wavelength or changes in the cavity length itself can inhibit lasing, and feedback interaction between the pump laser and the terahertz laser can affect stability. Therefore, designers must pay careful attention to all of these things to achieve reliable performance.

In the past, research groups often built their own OPTLs, which were typically large and extremely difficult to use and maintain. Today, OPTL laser systems are smaller and more reliable turnkey systems. These improved systems stem from several developments, including permanently sealed, single-mode, frequency-stabilized, folded-cavity, radio-frequency-excited waveguide CO_2 lasers; sealed FIR gas cells that eliminate gas transport issues; and exquisitely stable passive resonator structures. The integration of these various improved laser technologies into a truly operator-friendly system has ensured ease of use.

Indeed, OPTLs can operate at many discrete frequencies, ranging from less than 300 GHz (1,000 μm) to more than 10 THz (30 μm). Different molecular gases each have their own spectrum of available lines. Sideband generation technology can add instantaneous tunability to any of the available OPTL laser lines.

Other Terahertz Sources

Many other terahertz source technologies have been investigated in the past four decades. Numerous groups worldwide are producing tunable CW terahertz radiation using photomixing of near-IR lasers. For example, Gerald Fraser's group at the National Institute of Standards and Technology is frequency mixing the output of a near-IR, fixed-frequency diode laser with that of a tunable Ti:sapphire laser in a low-temperature-grown gallium arsenide photomixer fabricated with the appropriate antenna pattern. This approach yields tens of nanowatts of tunable output with a spectral content governed by the spectral content of the near-IR laser.

Backward-wave oscillators (BWOs) are electron tubes that can be used to generate tunable output at the long-wavelength end of the terahertz spectrum. To operate, however, they require a highly homogeneous magnetic field of approximately 10 kG.

Direct multiplied (DM) sources, such as those marketed by Virginia Diodes, Inc. (Charlottesville, VA), take millimeter-wave sources and directly multiply their output up to terahertz frequencies. DM sources with frequencies up to a little more than 1 THz and approximately 1 μW of output have been used as local oscillators for heterodyne receivers in select applications, most of which are in radio astronomy. However, they can produce substantially more output power at lower frequencies, and they are often well suited to applications requiring frequencies of less than 500 GHz.

In addition, physicists in Italy, Switzerland, the United States, and the United Kingdom have recently demonstrated quantum-cascade semiconductor lasers operating at wavelengths in the 4.4-THz regime. These lasers are made from 1,500 alternating layers (or stages) of gallium arsenide and aluminum gallium arsenide and have produced 2 mW of peak power (20 nW average power), and advances in output power and operating wavelength continue at a rapid pace. Applying a potential across the device causes electrons to cascade through each stage, emitting photons along the way. The photon wavelength is determined by the thickness of the stages. These lasers currently work best at only a few kelvins, but in the future they could become an important source of commercial terahertz systems . . .

The choice of a terahertz source will determine the type of detection scheme required. Sources with sub-milliwatt output power complicate detection and often necessitate the use of liquid-helium-cooled bolometers or similar devices. Short-pulse terahertz devices often need gated detection using a TDS switch.

For time-domain spectroscopy, or where an overall snapshot of the spectral characteristics of a sample in the terahertz region is important, TDS technology may be the optimal choice. For a more precise, higher-resolution look, consider the OPTL system, using either discrete frequencies or tunable sideband generation technology. Many applications do not need the complete terahertz spectrum of a sample but merely need to identify one or two characteristic features. In these cases, the OPTL system may be preferable to the TDS system because of its operational simplicity, high signal-to-noise ratio, and ability to use conventional, room-temperature detectors.

Although the practical application of terahertz radiation is in its infancy, the recent availability of reliable sources in the 0.3- to 5-THz range may have a wide-ranging impact on science, industry, and medicine. Short-pulse terahertz systems are used in time-domain spectroscopy to understand biological processes and to create two- and three-dimensional images. CW OPTL systems have been used extensively in aerospace and astronomical applications, primarily for remote sensing, and may find new uses as terahertz applications mature.

Reprinted with permission from "Terahertz Radiation: Applications and Sources," by Mueller, Eric R., *The Industrial Physicist*, August/September 2003, Vol. 9, No. 4, p. 27. © 2003, American Institute of Physics.

When the semiconductor transistor was invented in the late 1940s, it ushered in the beginning of a new era in technology, spurring advancements in innovation starting with the transistor radio and leading to the massive worldwide surge in computer accessibility and use. In order for this revolution to take place, sophisticated techniques for the manufacture of semiconductor devices were developed, and now those same techniques are being used to usher in a new kind of technological revolution—the revolution of the micro-machine. MEMS, or Microelectromechanical systems, are literally tiny machines on the scale of 1/1000 of a millimeter, which perform as clocks, springs, screws, mirrors, and many other components in a multitude of applications. In this article excerpt giving an overview of the MEMS revolution, researchers at Bell Labs, Lucent Technologies, and Agere Systems in Murray Hill, New Jersey, explain how MEMS can perform in a variety of applications, including as microphones and switching components in optical communication networks. —LCK

From "The Little Machines That Are Making It Big"
by David Bishop, Peter Gammel, and C. Randy Giles
Physics Today, October 2001

Imagine a world with machines the size of mites tending to all sorts of jobs. Some of them keep cars running smoothly and safely, saving hundreds of thousands of people from perishing in auto accidents. Other machines rout petabits (peta$=10^{15}$) of information each second, play movies downloaded from the World Wide Web, or perform scientific measurements of an unprecedented sensitivity and precision. Chip-sized chemical factories produce dangerous materials, but only when and where needed.

Such a world exists today: We live in it. It is the world of modern silicon micromechanics.[1] This world was anticipated with remarkable foresight by Richard Feynman more than 40 years ago, when transistors were a new and unproven technology and integrated circuits (ICs) were still many years into the future. In his 1959 talk, "There's Plenty of Room at the Bottom," published shortly thereafter,[2] Feynman suggested what micromachines could be, why one would want to use them, how to build them, and how physics for machines at the microscale would be different than for machines at the macroscale. Nowadays, it is possible to fabricate inexpensive micromachines that range in size from 0.1 to 100 microns, require little power, and operate at high speed. Such qualities make micromachines a compelling choice for a wide variety of applications. Micro-mechanics technology is profoundly changing the way we think about and use machines.

True Machines

The microscopic devices we are talking about are machines in the truest sense of the word. They have moving parts, sometimes millions of them. They can be as simple as cantilevers or as complicated as mechanical clocks. Elements such as rotary joints, springs, hinged plates, simple screws, suspended and unsuspended beams, diaphragms, mechanical striplines, and latches can be built and used reliably in a wealth of applications.

Micromachines, or microelectromechanical systems (MEMS), are made using a variety of techniques origi-nally developed for use in the $200-billion-per-year semiconductor industry. Sophisticated deposition tools, lithographic processes, wire bonders, photoresists, packages, Si wafers, modeling tools, and even reliability methodologies can be used in making MEMS devices. The benefit of being able to recycle existing technologies cannot be overestimated; recycling can be especially useful for those who design devices intended primarily for scientific applications, typically with almost no development funds.

The worldwide market for MEMS is estimated to exceed tens of billions of dollars in the next several years. In this article, we will focus on a number of key application areas: automobiles, handheld phones, dis-play technologies, lightwave systems, and scientific measurements.

Car Talk

An important, commercially successful MEMS device in widespread use today is the automotive airbag sensor,[3] which measures rapid deceleration of a car and triggers the explosive filling of an airbag. Before the use of a MEMS device in this application, airbags were typically triggered by an electromechanical device roughly the size of a can of soda, weighing several pounds and costing about $15. Now the same function is accomplished with a MEMS device that costs just a few dollars and is the size of a small cube of sugar. The smaller size of the MEMS device allows it to respond more quickly to rapid deceleration. As a consequence, it is now practical to have airbags in car doors to protect occupants against side impacts. MEMS airbag sensors have an additional important advantage over their macromechanical predecessors—integrated electronics that allow for self-testing. The test is initiated whenever a driver turns on the ignition, and its successful conclusion is indicated by an illuminated dashboard light.

Other applications for MEMS in automobiles include inertial sensors for keeping track of a car's location, tilt meters to warn of impending roll-overs, and pressure gauges used in the engine to assure proper and efficient operation. In the near future, MEMS devices will be key components of smart tires, which will remain properly inflated at all times. If tires are maintained with proper air pressure, not only will cars be safer, but, in addition, the US could reduce fuel consumption by an estimated 10%. Smart tires have microscopic pressure sensors as part of a feedback loop that includes a pump in the car. Thus, the responsibility of maintaining proper tire pressure rests with the car, not with the driver.

Automotive applications mark the beginning of a radically new technology. The airbag sensor in particular, with its better than 100 million device years of experience in the inhospitable environment of a car, has proved the reliability of this technology. The experience gained in the automotive arena can be used to guide the application of MEMS devices in other equally demanding environments.

Micro-Microphones

Modern handheld phones need to be small and inexpensive, and should not draw a lot of power. At the same time, they must be functional. These requirements are tailor-made for micromachines. MEMS devices are low power because they are typically electrostatically operated. They are small and can be easily integrated with both radio frequency analog circuits as well as digital circuits. Thus, one can build on-chip devices to replace large, off-chip components that require expensive interconnections to the rest of the circuit. Candidate devices for use in handheld phones include inductors, varactors (voltage-tunable capacitors), filters, tank circuits, RF switches, and micro-microphones.[4]

The micro-microphone . . . is an interesting example of such an on-chip device. In a typical cellular telephone, the microphone is large. At first, it seems a good candidate for miniaturization and integration with the Si electronics. But the disparity in size between the wavelength of sound and the size of MEMS devices suggests that MEMS micro-microphones would not work. The way around the difficulty is to use very sensitive readout electronics to compensate for the poor acoustic coupling.

On-chip microphones might make it possible to build radios on a chip. Or, it may be possible to use arrays of micro-microphones for acoustical source location to minimize coupling to extraneous noise sources—much as humans do with their two ears when having a conversation in a noisy room. MEMS devices are allowing acoustical engineers to accomplish tasks that were previously thought to require large and expensive equipment . . .

Switching the Light Fantastic

Not too long ago, many of us pointed to the telephone as a communications tool essential to our social and work lives. Now many of us cannot imagine living and working without the Internet. Photonics is the technology that makes the Internet possible: Almost every bit sent over the Internet is transmitted as light on optical fibers.

A typical lightwave system consists of optical fibers routed between major metropolitan areas. Data are usually sent over many different wavelengths of light on a single fiber because light is uncharged and the different colors are largely noninteracting in clean glass. The combining of several wavelengths of light on a single optical fiber is called WDM, or wavelength division multiplexing. More than a thousand separate wavelengths, or channels, can be transmitted on a single fiber.

The data capacity of fibers has been doubling every six to nine months. Impressive improvements in the transparency of glass optical fibers have allowed scientists and engineers to increase the data carrying rate of a single fiber to the previously unimaginable levels of more than 10^{13} bits per second. But the capacity to carry a great deal of data is not enough. Data need to be manipulated by, for example, being routed from one fiber to another. MEMS devices are part of the technology that will carry out such manipulations, allowing us to benefit from continuing increases in fibers' data capacity.

The sizes of MEMS devices make them well suited to optical applications. The wavelength of visible light is an appreciable fraction of a micron, comparable to the size of the smallest micromachines; a semiconductor laser has a length scale measured in tens of microns; and an optical fiber has a diameter of roughly 100 μm, comparable to large MEMS devices.

Simple MEMS devices include switches that take a single optical input and divert it to either of two outputs, and optical shutters, which simply block light from going downstream. More complex micromachines can adjust the spectral response of an optical amplifier much like the slide switches on a stereo adjust the acoustical frequency response to mix in more treble or bass. Even more complicated systems include add/drop multiplexers, which can route individual optical wavelengths in a fiber to desired destinations.

The applications for MEMS devices in lightwave systems[6, 7] range from variable optical attenuators, the optical equivalent of an electrical rheostat for adjusting the intensity of optical signals, to the application that launched a hundred startups—the complex optical crossconnect, also called an optical switch.

An optical switch routes data from one set of optical fibers to another at locations called nodes. With trillions of bits of data per second on a single fiber and hundreds to thousands of fibers entering and leaving a large node, the aggregate switching capacity needed can be enormous.

The standard way of switching the data was to convert the optical signals into electrical ones, use a large, fast electronic switch to route them, and then turn the signals back into light for transmission. Unfortunately, an electronic bottleneck has developed. The ability of fibers to transmit optical data has outstripped the ability of electronic devices to convert that data into electrical signals and switch it. The solution is all-optical switching—keeping the data as photons for both switching and transmission. Enter MEMS.

The basic idea with MEMS switches is to use microscopic mirrors to direct beams of light from many inputs to many outputs without slowing down the data streams by conversions from optical to electrical and back. Rerouting light with MEMS switches not only breaks the electronic bottleneck, it has many other advantages as well. It is data rate independent in the sense that a mirror's behavior is independent of how fast the light turns on and off. Likewise, a mirror's behavior is wavelength independent. MEMS switches are small and fast, use little power, and, above all else, are inexpensive.

When the optical switch is operating, light from an array of optical fibers is focused by an array of lenses so that the output of each fiber lands on its own mirror. Each mirror can tilt along two directions and steer the beam to any single output fiber located in another array of fibers. Switches, roughly the size of soccer balls, with more than 1000 input and 1000 output ports have already been built with a demonstrated aggregate capacity of more than two petabits/sec. To put that into perspective, if everyone on the planet were to simultaneously make a telephone call or to browse the Web, the total rate at which information is transferred would be roughly one petabit/sec. This gives some idea of the power and potential of the MEMS technology.

The market for optical switches is estimated to become more than $5 billion annually by the year 2005. That's why a large number of startups and established companies are working to develop these devices: There is a large pot of gold at the end of this particular rainbow . . .

A Lesson from an Old Radio

In this article we have given the reader a mere glimpse of what has been done with MEMS devices and what may be accomplished in the near future. It is clear to us that the field of micromechanics will change the paradigm of what machines are, how and where we use them, what they cost, and how we design them. It may not be an exaggeration to say that we are on the verge of a new industrial revolution driven by a new and completely different class of machines.

The invention of the transistor may prove a useful guide for what to expect. When first discovered, the transistor was used as a replacement for vacuum tubes in applications, like radios, where vacuum tubes worked well enough. One of us (DJB) recalls that, in 1960, he received as a birthday gift a transistor radio whose case proudly announced that the radio had six transistors. Six-transistor radios would have been easy to predict in 1947 when the transistor was invented. Today, however, we take for granted microprocessors with tens of millions of transistors. No one in 1947 could have predicted such a thing and what it would do to our world.

We currently use micromachines to do things that in most cases can be done by macromachines. (The micromachines, however, do a better job.) In 20 or 30 years, though, society will be using micromachines in ways impossible for us to imagine today. Those of us working in the field of micromechanics look forward to helping make it happen.

References

1. For a general reference on micromachines in a wide range of applications, see the special issue on "Microelectromechanical Systems: Technology and Applications" *MRS Bull.* 26 (April 2001).
2. R. Feynman, *Eng. Sci.* 23, 22 (1960).
3. T. A. Core, W. K. Tsang, S. J. Sherman, *Solid State Technol.* 36, 39 (1993).
4. D. J. Young, *MRS Bull.* 26, 331 (2001).
6. C. R. Giles et al., *MRS Bull.* 26, 328 (2001).
7. D. Bishop et al., *Sci. Am.* 284, 88 (January 2001).

Web Sites

Due to the changing nature of Internet links, the Rosen Publishing Group, Inc., has developed an online list of Web sites related to the subject of this book. This site is updated regularly. Please use this link to access the list:

http://www.rosenlinks.com/cdfp/soew

For Further Reading

The American Institute of Physics Bulletin of Physics News. "Physics News Update." Retrieved October 19, 2004 (http://www.aip.org/physnews/update).

Beranek, L. *Concert Halls and Opera Houses: Music, Acoustics, and Architecture*. 2nd Edition. New York, NY: Springer-Verlag, 2004.

Boggess, Albert, and Francis J. Narcowich. *A First Course in Wavelets with Fourier Analysis*. Upper Saddle River, NJ: Prentice Hall, 2001.

Bromley, D. Allan. *A Century of Physics*. New York, NY: Springer-Verlag, 2002.

Cheeke, J. David N. *Fundamentals and Applications of Ultrasonic Wave*. Boca Raton, FL: CRC Press, 2002.

Ehrlich, Robert. *Nine Crazy Ideas in Science: A Few Might Even Be True*. Princeton, NJ: Princeton University Press, 2001.

Ketchum, Mark. "Bridge Collapse Page." Retrieved October 19, 2004 (http://www.ketchum.org/bridgecollapse.html).

Lynch, D. K., and W. Livingston. *Color and Light in Nature*. 2nd Edition. Cambridge, England: Cambridge University Press, 2001.

Johnston, Ian. *Measured Tones: The Interplay of Physics and Music*. Bristol, England: Institute of Physics Publishing, 2001.

Jones, Douglas Samuel. *Acoustic and Electromagnetic Waves*. Oxford, England: Oxford University Press, 1989.

Mallinckrodt, A. John. "Animations: A Small Collection of Physics-Related Animations." Retrieved October 19, 2004 (http://www.csupomona.edu/~ ajm/ materials/animations.html).

Meissner, R. *The Little Book of Planet Earth*. New York, NY: Copernicus Books, 2002.

Park, David. *The Fire Within the Eye: A Historical Essay on the Nature and Meaning of Light*. Cambridge, England: Princeton University Press, 1999.

Ratner, Mark A., and Daniel Ratner. *Nanotechnology: A Gentle Introduction to the Next Big Idea*. 1st Edition. Upper Saddle River, NJ: Prentice Hall, 2002.

Saslow, Wayne M. *Concepts Before Equations— Electricity, Magnetism, and Light*. New York, NY: Academic Press, 2002.

Bibliography

Addison, Paul. "The Little Wave with the Big Future." *Physics World*, March 2004, pp. 35–39.

Bishop, David, Peter Gammel, and C. Randy Giles. "The Little Machines That Are Making It Big." *Physics Today*, October 2001, pp. 38–44.

Cooper, Martin. "Antennas Get Smart." *Scientific American*, July 2003, pp. 49–55.

Dutton, Zachary, Naomi S. Ginsberg, Christopher Slowe, and Lene Vestergaard Hau. "The Art of Taming Light: Ultra-Slow and Stopped Light." *Europhysics News*, March/April 2004, p. 33.

Feldman, Bernard J. "What to Say About the Tacoma Narrows Bridge to Your Introductory Physics Class." *Physics Teacher*, February 2003, pp. 92–96.

Fishbane, Paul M., Stephen Gasiorowicz, and Stephen T. Pearson. *Physics for Scientists and Engineers (Extended Version)*. Englewood Cliffs, NJ: Pearson Higher Education, 1993.

Gammon, Daniel, and Duncan G. Steel. "Optical Studies of Single Quantum Dots." *Physics Today*, October 2002, p. 36.

Garrett, Steven L., and Scott Backhaus. "The Power of Sound." *American Scientist*, November/December 2000, pp. 516–525.

Gerstein, Edmund R. "Manatees, Bioacoustics and Boats." *American Scientist*, March/April 2002, pp. 154–163.

Giancoli, Douglas C. *Physics for Scientists and Engineers*. 3rd Edition. Upper Saddle River, NJ: Prentice Hall, 2000.

Hall, Donald E. *Musical Acoustics*. 3rd Edition. Pacific Grove, CA: Brooks/Cole, 2002.

Hardwick, John. "The Subtlety of Rainbows." *Physics World*, February 2004, pp. 29–33.

Kaczkowski, Peter. "Supersonic Boom for Ultrasound." *Physics World*, July 2004, p. 19.

Lafon, Cyril, David Melodelima, Jean-Yves Chapelon, and Dominique Cathignol. "Destroying Deep-Seated Tumors with 'Interstitial' Ultrasound." Acoustical Society of America Lay Language paper, 147th Acoustical Society of America Meeting, May 25, 2004.

Lay, Thorne, Quentin Williams, and Edward J. Garnero. "The Core-Mantle Boundary Layer and Deep Earth Dynamics." *Nature*, April 2, 1998, pp. 461–468.

Liu, Lanbo, and Donald G. Albert. "A Shot in the City: Locating a Sound Source in an Urban Environment." Acoustical Society of America Lay Language paper, 147th Acoustical Society of America Meeting, May 28, 2001.

Lohse, Detlof. "Sonoluminescence: Inside a Micro-Reactor." *Nature*, July 25, 2002, pp. 381–383.

LoPresto, Michael C., and Rachel McKay. "Detecting Our Own Solar System from Afar." *The Physics Teacher*, April 2004, p. 208.

Mueller, Eric R. "Terahertz Radiation: Applications and Sources." *The Industrial Physicist*, August/September 2003, pp. 27–29.

Muir, Hazel. "Bursting with Energy." *New Scientist*, March 9, 2002, pp. 4–5.

Ouellette, Jennifer. "Seeing with Sound." *Industrial Physicist*, June/July 2004, pp. 14–17.

Ouellette, Jennifer. "Time-Resolved Spectroscopy Comes of Age." *Industrial Physicist*, February/March 2004, pp. 16–19.

Parker, Greg G., and M. Charlton. "Photonic Crystals." *Physics World*, August 2000, pp. 29–34.

Paul, Clayton R., Keith W. Whites, and Syed A. Nasar. *Introduction to Electromagnetic Fields*. 3rd Edition. Boston, MA: WCB/McGraw-Hill, 1998.

Pendry, John B., and David R. Smith. "Reversing Light with Negative Refraction." *Physics Today*, June 2004, pp. 37–43.

Ramsayer, Kate. "Infrasonic Symphony: The Greatest Sounds Never Heard." *Science News*, January 10, 2004, pp. 26–28.

Rothstein, Edward. "If Music Is the Architect . . ." *New York Times*, May 22, 2004, p. B7.

Seddon, N., and T. Bearpark. "Observation of the Inverse Doppler Effect." *Science*, November 2003, pp. 1537–1540.

Senturia, Stephen. *Microsystem Design*. Norwell, MA: Kluwar Academic Publishers, 2001.

Index

About the Editor

Dr. L. C. Krysac is a physics researcher, writer, and teacher with more than ten years of experience teaching students at the undergraduate level. Since receiving her Ph.D. in physics from the University of Toronto, she has been a postdoctoral researcher at Pennsylvania State University, in State College, Pennsylvania, and an assistant professor at the University of the Pacific in Stockton, California, where she taught upper-division electromagnetism and the physics of music for several years. Her research focuses on the physics of fracture. She is currently on sabbatical in Toronto, Canada, writing science articles and working on several other writing projects.

Photo Credits

Front cover (clockwise from top right): "Infinite Textures," © Comstock Images Royalty free division; wave refraction experiment courtesy of John Pendry; "Liquid Crystal," © Getty Images; background image of gyroscope © Getty Images; portrait, Isaac Newton © Library of Congress, Prints and Photographs Division. Back cover: top image "Electrons Orbiting Nucleus" © Royalty-Free/Corbis; bottom: Liquid Crystal © Getty Images.

Designer: Geri Fletcher; Editor: Kathy Kuhtz Campbell